second edition

In-Line Skating

Mark Powell
John Svensson

Human Kinetics

Library of Congress Cataloging-in-Publication Data

Powell, Mark, 1959-
    In-Line Skating / Mark Powell, John Svensson. -- 2nd ed.
     p. cm.
    Includes index.
    ISBN 0-88011-659-5
    1. In-line skating. I. Svensson, John. II. Title.
    GV859.73.P69   1997   97-16811
    796.21—dc21   CIP

ISBN: 0-88011-695-5

Acquisitions Editor: Martin Barnard; **Developmental Editor:** Elaine Mustain; **Assistant Editors:** Susan Moore-Kruse, Sandra Merz Bott, Melinda Graham; **Editorial Assistants:** Amy Carnes, Laura Majersky, Jennifer Hemphill; **Copyeditor:** Jacqueline Blakley; **Proofreader:** Sarah Wiseman; **Indexer:** Craig Brown; **Graphic Designer:** Judy Henderson; **Graphic Artist:** Yvonne Winsor; **Photo Editor:** Boyd LaFoon; **Cover Designer:** Jack Davis; **Photographer (cover):** John Kelly; **Photographers (interior):** David Robbins, except as noted by photos; **Illustrator:** Tom Roberts; **Printer:** United Graphics

Human Kinetics books are available at special discounts for bulk purchase. Special editions or book excerpts can also be created to specification. For details, contact the Special Sales Manager at Human Kinetics.

Printed in the United States of America   10 9 8 7 6 5 4 3 2 1

Human Kinetics
Web site: http://www.humankinetics.com/

United States: Human Kinetics
P.O. Box 5076
Champaign, IL 61825-5076
1-800-747-4457
e-mail: humank@hkusa.com

Canada: Human Kinetics, Box 24040
Windsor, ON N8Y 4Y9
1-800-465-7301 (in Canada only)
e-mail: humank@hkcanada.com

Europe: Human Kinetics, P.O. Box IW14
Leeds LS16 6TR, United Kingdom
(44) 1132 781708
e-mail: humank@hkeurope.com

Australia: Human Kinetics
57A Price Avenue
Lower Mitcham, South Australia 5062
(08) 277 1555
e-mail: humank@hkaustralia.com

New Zealand: Human Kinetics
P.O. Box 105-231, Auckland 1
(09) 523 3462
e-mail: humank@hknewz.com

To Jo,

Thanks for your love and support.

Mark Powell

And to

Gunde, Anika, Larson, and Mikaella: junior skaters and future champions.

John Svensson

ACKNOWLEDGMENTS

A sincere thanks to K2 Skates and Leading Edge Sports—Northwest representatives for Rollerblade and Hyper Wheels—for sharing their products and photographs; to members of the Washington In-Line Skating Association—Patricia Ann Bottcher, Polly Stewart, and Jason Stewart—for modeling in the instructional photographs; to Jenny Campbell from Anderson's Greenlake Nautilus for modeling in the stretching photographs; to David Robbins for his talented photographic work; to Yvette Svensson and Melinda Miller for their tremendous patience and without whom this book would not be complete; many, many thanks to Tony Meibock and Hank Miller for all their help; and a special thanks to Martin Barnard and Elaine Mustain of Human Kinetics Publishers whose guidance led us to a better second edition: Without their dedication this book would not have happened.

CONTENTS

PREFACE

Welcome to the world of in-line skating! You are about to enjoy an exciting form of physical exercise that is as fun as it is worthwhile. You are not alone in your interest: In-line skating has grown from an almost unknown sport in 1985 to one of the top 20 participation sports today. The National Sporting Goods Association estimates that in-line skating participation has jumped 512 percent since 1991. As a recreational skater, in-line instructor, and freelance writer (Powell) and one of the industry's top skate designers and professional racers (Svensson), we are well-suited to cover the various aspects of in-line skating and will give you solid, fundamental instruction.

The first edition of *In-Line Skating* was a tremendous success. In this new and updated edition, you'll find the latest information on equipment, the sport's development, and techniques. Whether you're a beginning, intermediate, or advanced skater, you will find information useful for learning or refining the skills that will help you skate safely and confidently.

If you are interested in running, skiing, cycling, aggressive skating, dance skating, racing, or simply jumping in a pair of lightweight ski boots on wheels, *In-Line Skating* will help you combine the benefits of a low-impact, highly aerobic workout with an adrenaline rush that will keep you coming back for more.

This book is divided into three parts. Part I provides you with what you need to know before strapping on a pair of in-line skates. You'll learn how to select appropriate skates for any type of skating and how to tell the difference between quality skates and toy skates. You'll learn what safety gear you need and how to wear it. You'll also find out how to stretch and warm up before you skate in order to avoid muscle injuries.

Part II includes 32 photographs and diagrams with step-by-step instructions on the fundamentals of in-line skating. Drills and tips for correcting errors are included to assist you in perfecting your skills. Proper posture is the key to steady balance, and you'll see the right and wrong ways to stand. After reading *In-Line Skating*, you'll understand why stroke, glide, stroke, glide is better than stroke, stroke, stroke. You'll find the answer to in-line skating's most frequently asked question, How do you stop these things? Then, after learning each technique, you'll discover how to put it all together into a smooth, confident style.

If you decide to get more serious, Part III introduces you to racing, aggressive skating, and roller hockey. We take you through the training steps for in-line racing, from completing 10K races to skating marathons. You'll take a peek into the outrageous world of aggressive skating, and we'll answer some common questions. *In-Line Skating* teaches you the fundamentals of the popular team sport of roller hockey and provides the resources to help you form a team and league in your area.

In short, *In-Line Skating* is the most comprehensive, well-organized, in-depth discussion of the sport ever published. We have provided a solid foundation on which you can build your in-line skating skills, and we have introduced ways for you to utilize those skills. Whether training for serious athletic competition, participating for health and recreation, or seeking your next extreme sports adventure, take time to read, learn, and practice. The time you invest with this book now will pay off for many years to come.

We have tried to include photographs that depict skaters wearing full safety gear. However, in some photographs the skaters are wearing only partial or no safety gear. These skaters all have an advanced skill level and are taking additional risk of injury. We encourage you to always wear all safety gear as described in chapter 2.

BEFORE YOU SKATE

In Part I, we will introduce you to in-line skating and its benefits, and examine skating and protective gear. We'll also have an in-depth discussion about pre-skate considerations.

If you already have your skates and safety gear and are anxious to get started, you can skip ahead to chapter 3 for some pre-skate warm-up stretching.

CHAPTER 1

INTRODUCTION TO IN-LINE SKATING

©K2/Scott Markewitz

In-line skating, one of the most popular participant sports in the world, has developed in many different directions since its contemporary beginnings in the early 1980s. Recreational enthusiasts, racers, aggressive skaters, and roller hockey players have found that in-line skating is an inexpensive, fun, and healthy sport.

In-line skating as a sport has taken on an identity of its own and is attracting participants from many segments of our society. It has become a part of our everyday lives, represented regularly in the media and on streets, sidewalks, trails, and campuses around the world. Everyone from Grandma to Princess Di is in-line skating.

Millions of people have found in-line skating to be a great form of exercise and a healthy workout. It is a low-impact, highly aerobic form of exercise that burns calories and tones and shapes thighs and buttocks.

WHAT'S IN A NAME?

In-line skating is often referred to as rollerblading, and in-line skates are referred to as rollerblades. The name originated with Rollerblade, Inc., of Minneapolis, MN, the manufacturer who developed the modern in-line skate and remains one of the top manufacturers of skating equipment. But in-line skating has diversified over the last several years, and many other manufacturers have entered the market, so it is inaccurate to call the sport rollerblading. As a reflection of this, in 1991, the Rollerblade In-Line Skate Association changed its name to the International In-Line Skating Association (IISA). Since that time, the sport has been referred to as in-line skating.

IT'S EASIER THAN YOU THINK

In-line skating looks hard. After all, you have to move while balancing on a thin line of wheels. Many people remember the sore ankles they got trying to learn to ice skate. The apparent similarity of ice skates and in-line skates might cause you to expect pain and frustration in learning to in-line skate.

Surprisingly, however, in-line skating is easier than ice skating or even roller skating. This ease is a result of the hard-shell, ski-type boot on in-line skates. These boots provide outstanding ankle support and make it relatively easy to stand up on in-line skates. Even soft-boot skates have some type of support system beyond fabric or leather to keep you on your feet.

The wheels on in-line skates are also a factor in the ease of skating. Modern urethane wheels are quite different from skateboard and roller skate wheels of generations past. Today's wheels are sticky and resilient at the same time. The stickiness keeps the wheels from slipping and sliding out from under you while stroking or turning. The resilience allows wheels to roll easily over pebbles, cracks, and other obstacles in your path. The high quality of modern wheels makes in-line skates stable.

The stability of in-line skates is also increased by the length of the wheel base. If you were to compare the length of the wheel base on traditional roller skates with that of in-line skates, you would find that the in-line skate wheel base is at least 1 to 2 inches longer for the same size boot (see figure 1.1). This additional length adds a great deal of front-to-back stability.

a   b

FIGURE 1.1   Both skates are for the same foot size. The wheel base of the in-line skate (b) is 2 inches longer than that of the quad skate (a).

5

Although in-line skating is easier than many people think, that doesn't mean it is without challenges. It still takes instruction, time, and practice to become a proficient skater.

THE EVOLUTION OF IN-LINE SKATING

The concept of putting skate wheels in a line instead of side-by-side is not a new one (see figure 1.2). Louis Legrange created a pair of in-line skates in 1849 to simulate an ice skating scene in the French opera *Le Prophète*. This was the first time in-line skates were used successfully, but because one could not turn or stop in the skates, they were considered a novelty rather than a practical invention.

© Library of Congress

FIGURE 1.2   William Fuller took his comic skating act to India, Egypt, and Russia in the 1860s.

Modern in-line skates were developed in Minnesota in the early 1980s when a group of ice hockey players made them to help them train during the off-season. The hard-shell boot and urethane wheels proved to be great improvements on Louis Legrange's design, and the skates worked. From that beginning, the sport grew and attracted the interest of athletes. Before long, nonathletes were skating on in-lines, too, just for the fun of it.

Athletes from a variety of sports fueled the initial growth of the sport with their desire to cross-train on in-line skates. Ice hockey players and cross-country and Alpine skiers led the way by realizing the advantages of off-season training on in-line skates. They were soon followed by runners, cyclists, and roller skaters who saw the benefits of a low-impact, highly aerobic, fun workout.

As previously mentioned, skating today is a multifaceted sport with a huge group of recreational skaters of all ages and experience levels. In addition, the sport is developing many different special-interest groups. These include racers, roller hockey players, aggressive skaters, and figure skaters.

Today there are as many types of skates as there are types of skating. Skates are being built for children, adult recreation, cross-training, hockey, racing, aggressive skating, and figure skating. There are various types of wheels and accessories as well. A variety of these products are introduced and reviewed in chapter 2.

SKATING FOR FITNESS

Medical research has shown that exercising three or more times per week will improve our lives in many ways. Exercise slows the aging process, reduces the risk of heart disease, controls weight, and reduces stress. In-line skating is a great way to exercise, and it adds another benefit that many other forms of exercise lack: fun!

In-line skating is a low-impact, highly aerobic workout. The stroke, recovery, and glide of in-line skating works different muscle groups than other forms of exercise and is easier on the body's joints. In-line skating is one of the few forms of aerobic exercise that, because of its distinctive side-to-side skating motion, works both the inner and outer thigh muscles, which are typically hard to tone.

One of the most common questions asked about any aerobic exercise is, "How many calories does it burn?" According to research done by Dr. Carl Foster of the University of Wisconsin Medical School, an in-line skater working at a vigorous pace will burn approximately 570 calories an hour. This is an average determined by measuring several people ranging in fitness level, gender, and weight. An in-line skater who is skating at a moderate pace will burn approximately 375 calories per hour.

CROSS-TRAINING ON IN-LINE SKATES

Athletes from many other sports have turned to in-line skating as a cross-training workout. The physical demands of in-line skating are similar to those of a variety of other sports in terms of coordination, muscles used, and cardiovascular conditioning. And the fun and excitement of in-line skating offer a welcome break in routine training for other sports. In this section we will take a close look at the benefits of cross-training on in-line skates for alpine skiing, cross-country skiing, cycling, and running.

ALPINE SKIING

The Alpine skier who wants to hit the slopes in shape each winter should take a close look at the benefits of in-line skating. Whether your skiing interests are in recreational, freestyle, slalom, or racing, the benefits of in-line skating during the off-season are great. The combination of speed, power, and acceleration you feel while carving a turn on in-line skates feels closer than anything else to skiing (see figure 1.3).

Major muscle groups such as thighs, hamstrings, buttocks, hips, groin, and low back all receive a tremendous workout when applying alpine skiing techniques to in-line skates. Maintaining a regular schedule of skating during the off-season will do wonders for most skiers.

a   b

FIGURE 1.3   The body posture and position of the skier (a) while executing a turn is almost the same as that of an in-line skater (b).

If your skiing interests are specific, you will easily discover cross-training techniques that will complement your interests. Ski racers may want to set up a series of cones or gates to simulate a race course. Freestyle skiers can simulate their disciplines through jumps or ballet and tricks on skates.

CROSS-COUNTRY SKIING

Cross-country skiers will find that in-line skating closely approximates the motion of their sport. If you compare an in-line skater side-by-side with a cross-country skier, you will see that many of the motions are nearly identical (see figure 1.4).

a   b

FIGURE 1.4   The stroke leg and glide leg position of the cross-country skier (a) and in-line skater (b) are nearly identical.

Many cross-country skiers use their ski poles while on in-line skates and work out in hilly terrain. The combination of poles and hills will give a better upper-body and cardiovascular workout because of the increased muscle usage and demand for more oxygen from the heart and lungs.

Ski poles are not recommended in areas where there are large numbers of pedestrians or cyclists, especially if you don't have much experience using them.

CYCLING

In-line skating can provide high speeds and racing conditions that are similar to bike racing. An in-line skater will get a slightly better cardiovascular workout, over similar terrain, than a cyclist. Initially, athletes who visually compare skating and cycling might believe that a skater who is gliding between strokes is resting, the same as a cyclist who is not pedaling. However, the skater must use more muscles to battle gravity and balance on one skate than the biker who is connected to a bike at five points. In addition, the cyclist has the benefit of changing gears on varying terrain. Therefore, a cross-training cyclist can build more muscle strength on skates than on a bike.

RUNNING

Runners who have experienced physical difficulties as a result of the high-impact conditions of their sport will find great relief with in-line skating. In-line skating provides a slightly less intense cardiovascular workout than running, but the demands on the body's joints are greatly reduced. Runners who desire to cross-train should include workouts that duplicate their running workout in terms of maintaining a similar heart rate for a similar amount of time. Obviously, when skating you will cover more miles because of higher speeds.

GO FOR IT!

The evidence is in. In-line skating is fun, exciting, and good for you! Let's get started. In the following chapters you'll learn how to find the equipment that's right for you, including safety gear. You'll find out what to do before you start skating and where to skate. Then step-by-step (or stroke-by-stroke), you'll learn how to in-line skate.

After getting a handle on the basics, you'll learn about advanced in-line skating and have an opportunity to see if you want to pursue one or more of the special niches of in-line skating.

So what are you waiting for? Go for it!

CHAPTER 2

SKATING EQUIPMENT

Keeping up with the development of new products for in-line skating can be a formidable challenge. As the relatively new sport develops, more products are being made to serve the needs of the participants. Today you can find everything from sophisticated skates for special-interest groups to shorts with hip pads sewn in to help avoid bruises when you fall. With the development of specialty equipment for niches within the in-line market, the proliferation of new products is over-whelming. Each year, manufacturers are getting better at addressing the specific needs of these growing niches within the sport which include:

- Recreational
- Fitness
- Cross-training
- Aggressive/stunt
- Hockey (also called roller hockey)
- Race

In this chapter we will look at the key pieces of in-line equipment and discuss things you should consider before making your buying decisions.

BEFORE YOU BUY

One way manufacturers and retailers of in-line skates have helped fuel the growth of skating is supporting rental and demonstration programs. In most major cities around the United States you can find a business that offers rental or free demonstration of in-line skates and related equipment.

These rental and demonstration programs are a great way to test the sport and various types of skates. The downside is that often the skates used in rental programs are inexpensive models with poor-quality wheels and bearings. Although such skates are safer for the beginner than high-quality models because they don't roll as fast, they will not give you a fair representation of the quality or performance of in-line skates in general. In spite of these deficiencies, beginning skaters can usually assess their true interest in the sport by first renting skates. Also, shops often will apply any rental fees toward the purchase of a pair of skates.

If you are interested in testing various skates for the purpose of making a buying decision, see whether the retailer has a demonstration pair of the exact model that you are considering purchasing. There can be tremendous differences in performance among models.

If testing skates represents your first experience on in-line skates, take time to read the following chapters on fundamental skating skills. Give special attention to the section in this chapter on safety gear and later to the rules of the road (see chapter 3); we cannot emphasize enough the importance of this information. As a beginning skater you will be susceptible to injury, so don't take a casual attitude toward getting on skates the first time. Skate smart.

COMPONENTS OF IN-LINE SKATES

In-line skates are made up of many different parts. In this section we will look at each of these components and examine how they affect the performance of the skate and the skater.

BOOTS

There are several aspects of boots that you need to think about as you choose skates. The construction can be either hard or soft, and closure systems, boot height, liners, and footbeds all vary by brand and model.

Hard or Soft?

Two basic types of boot construction are available on the market—hard shell and soft boot (see figures 2.6 and 2.7 on pages 31 and 32). Most boots are constructed with two pieces of molded plastic and are referred to as hard shell. The lower half of the boot covers the lower portion of the foot, much like an alpine ski boot. The upper half wraps around and supports the ankle. The upper and lower sections are connected on each side of the ankle with a hinge system that allows the ankle and boot to flex forward as the ankle would flex naturally.

The second and more modern category of boot construction is called soft boot. While the hard-shell boots described before contain a removable inner liner similar to an alpine ski boot, soft boots (available from a growing number of manufacturers) are made more like a hiking boot, with an external (and sometimes internal) cuff to provide support. Hard-shell boots use the exterior support shell to cover generally four sizes. In other words, a boot may be a size 9 to 10, but the exterior shell will fit liners in half-size increments (9, 9 1/2, 10, 10 1/2). On the other hand, soft boots, like hiking and athletic footwear, are available in half-sizes with no inner liner. Because of this, many people feel that soft boots provide better fit and performance. In addition, soft boots are generally more lightweight and breathable than hard-shell boots. Ultimately, however, it's a matter of personal preference. We recommend that you look at both hard-shell and soft-boot skates, then decide which one suits you better. Don't buy skates without at the very least—trying them on—or better yet, take them for a test spin. You are the only one who can decide which skates are best for you.

Closure Systems

A good closure system should provide good heel support while avoiding pressure points. If your foot slides around within the boot, performance is diminished and nasty blisters can result. Look for closure systems that allow a great degree of flexibility and adjustability without creating pressure points.

Most hard-shell boots use buckles or a combination of laces and buckles to secure the foot. Closure systems for hard boots can also vary by niche. For example, Velcro straps used by aggressive skaters seeking greater support than normal are widely used within both the hard-shell and soft-boot markets. Lace systems with hard-shell boots can often be difficult to adjust and work against ease of donning and doffing; thus buckle systems predominate within the hard-shell market.

Soft boots are generally secured with laces. In some soft-boot models, there is also a top-line buckle that is used to hold the foot securely in place and to provide ankle support.

Power straps, either across the saddle (that is, over the instep of the foot) or at the very top of the boot above the buckle, are enhancements that really help to hold the foot in place. Power straps, incidentally, come as original equipment in some skates, but they can be purchased separately and added to any skates that you buy.

Boot Height

The height of the boot is, generally speaking, directly related to the niche for which the boot was created. Higher cuffs provide more support and less flexibility (that is, less forward lean) than lower cuffs or no cuffs at all. For recreational boots, the cuff-and-boot height is generally high, in the range of 3 to 4 inches above the ankle. Fitness skates, in many cases, have what are called midheight cuffs, which are 1 to 2 inches lower than recreational cuffs. Cross-training skates vary—they can be as high as recreational boots or as low as a midheight fitness skate. Hockey skates have internal support systems in most cases and therefore have no exterior cuff at all. The boot height of hockey skates is the same as in customary ice hockey skates and recreational skates, coming 3 to 4 inches above the ankle joint. Stunt skate cuffs fall right between recreational high cuffs and fitness midheight cuffs. Race skates have either a very low cuff or no cuff at all. These skates have the lowest profile of all in-line skates, offer the least amount of support, and are the most difficult to skate on.

Liners

Soft boots do not have removable liners; they have internal support from a material called *heat-moldable thermoplastic.* These skates will break in a bit with use, but to overcome any fitting problems that might remain, they can be heated up and then custom formed to your foot. This procedure should only be done with the assistance of a specialty store retailer. Or contact the boot manufacturer to be sure you don't ruin your new pair of skates! The liner of the hard-shell boot is similar to that of a ski boot but is not as thick or insulating. These liners provide more support and comfort, when fitted correctly, than the traditional ice-skate or roller-skate boot.

The majority of liners are constructed from high-density foam surrounded by a nylon cloth.

One advantage of hard-shell boots over soft boots is that the liners are removable. Many liners are washable, so consider that when buying if your feet sweat a lot during exercise. Liners can be customized by building up the interior with foam pads for narrow feet or heating and stretching the plastic boot shells for wide feet. Custom fitting should be done only by qualified experts. It's easy to ruin a new pair of skates if you're not familiar with the correct procedures.

Footbeds

Footbeds are also referred to as innersoles, innersocks, and even orthotics by retailers and manufacturers. Footbeds rest underneath your foot and are generally made of a foam material covered by cloth. The simplest and most basic footbed has only the impression of cloth pressed onto the surface of the foam material and is in fact nothing more than foam material. (Look closely. Don't be fooled!) The high-end orthotics are made of many components: a plush cloth liner under your foot, a foam footbed under the cloth, different density foam under the forefoot, and even a plastic material around the heel to provide enhanced support. You need to be sure that your skates have a footbed to provide support and comfort. When buying a pair of skates, remove the footbed from the skate and examine it. Compare this footbed to that of the other skates you are considering. If you like the skates but hate the footbed, you can buy a better footbed separately.

FRAMES

The frame of an in-line skate is attached to the bottom of the boot and holds the wheels on the skate. On most skates the frame is a separate component that is attached to the boot with rivets or a similar attachment system. On some inexpensive skates the boot and frame are molded as one piece.

The Wheel Size a Frame Can Fit

One crucial consideration when looking at frames is the maximum wheel size your frame can accommodate. Most inexpensive skates can only take a maximum size 70 mm or 72 mm wheel. As you progress in your skating skill, you will likely want to upgrade the size of your wheels for better roll and more speed. When evaluating skates and frames, investigate the maximum wheel size that the skate you are buying can accommodate. Remember that, other than for stunt skates, some of which can only accommodate the smallest of wheels, it is best to choose skates with frames that can accommodate wheel sizes up to 80 mm to 82 mm. (For a discussion of wheel sizes and your type of skating, please see pages 22–24.)

Construction Materials

In general, there are three materials from which frames are made: plastic, metal, and composites.

Plastic frames. Most frames are constructed from molded plastic. When examining frames on skates, look for the stiffest frame possible. A stiff frame will translate your energy into pushing power. If your frame bends when you push off, you will have to work harder to gain speed, and you will ultimately have less control over your skates. The best plastic frames, although made of nylon, should also have some amount of glass fiber to provide stiffness.

There is no uniform method for testing frame stiffness. Experienced skate makers can twist frames in their hands and properly assess stiffness. You may be able to do the same eventually, but it will take some practice. Probably the quickest way to check stiffness is to remove the front wheel and all of the front wheel hardware. Now try to pinch the two rails of the frame together. The harder it is to pinch the two rails together, the greater the frame stiffness. Compare different brands. This will give you a reasonable relative indication of frame stiffness. Also look for cross-bracing, an effective feature in stiffening frames.

Plastic frames currently are preferred by most aggressive street skaters where grinding (a trick you'll learn about in chapter 10) is the main event. Although plastic frames are in many cases more than adequate, most other skaters (even aggressive ramp skaters, who often opt for aluminum frames) prefer more esoteric (read: more expensive) frame materials.

The elite in each category choose specific materials that meet their needs, and the masses seem to emulate the best.

Metal frames. A frame made of metal is not necessarily stiffer or more durable than a well-made plastic frame. Metal frames are primarily used by hockey enthusiasts and race skaters who seek the most direct transfer of energy to the ground. Make sure the frames you buy are made from metal either extruded or cut from a block and not die cast. You can't tell by looking at it; ask the shop employee or check the literature that comes with the skate. Look for cross-bracing on the frame, under the wheels (this applies to plastic frames as well). Metal frames can offer the direct energy transfer that you seek, but they also transfer bumps on the road right back up into the foot and can be uncomfortable over the long haul.

Composite frames. By composite frames we mean those esoteric and extremely expensive frames made by pressing resins into woven fiberglass, carbon, and even Kevlar sheets. These sheets are pressed into U-shaped, channel-like frames that are then mounted on skates. These frames in many cases can offer great stiffness and direct energy transfer to the pavement. In addition, composite frames have the advantage that they can often effectively dampen some of the vibration that travels up from the road and into your feet.

Frame Length

The length of the frame is measured from the center of the front axle to the center of the rear axle. The length of a frame can vary from 10 inches to 16 inches depending on the size of the boot and the type of skating for which it will be used (see figure 2.1). The most common frame length is 12 inches, found on most recreational and hockey skates. Longer frames are used on racing skates for more stability, and shorter frames are used for skates with small boot sizes.

WHEELS

There are more variables that affect performance in wheels than perhaps in any other component of skates. As you become a more proficient skater, these characteristics become

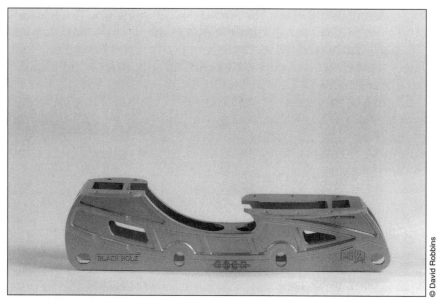

a

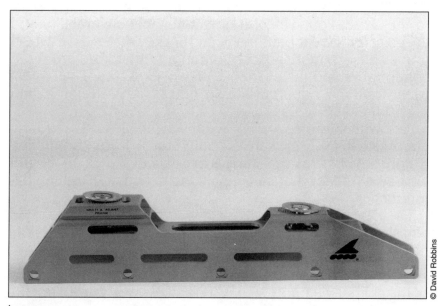

b

FIGURE 2.1 These two photos show the difference in length between a recreational skate frame (a) and a racing skate frame (b).

increasingly important. A speed skater will use a different kind of wheel on an outdoor road course than on an indoor, smooth, hardwood floor. The same is true for a hockey player. The selection of wheels can dramatically affect the skates' performance.

Choosing the right wheels to match your skating style can seem like a complex process, and there is not always one right wheel. The following sections describe the various components and characteristics of wheels and will help steer you in the right direction.

Number of Wheels

The number of wheels that are mounted on an in-line frame can vary depending on the intended use of the skates, the size of the frame, and the size of the skater's foot. Most standard skates have four wheels, some small skates have three wheels, and most speed skates have five wheels. More wheels will add stability in the front-to-back direction of the skates, but will reduce the side-to-side turning ability and add weight to the skate. Four-wheel frames offer maneuverability and are great for recreational, stunt, and hockey skates. Five-wheel frames absorb more road vibration and therefore are more comfortable and faster than four-wheel skates. Five-wheel frames are most appropriate for fitness, cross-training, and race skates.

Five-wheel frames are not readily available and are found almost exclusively in skate specialty stores. If you cannot find a store in your area that carries five-wheel skates, try to find a catalog retailer that can supply them. Or try searching the Internet.

Wheel Size

Wheel size, like nearly every other component we have discussed in this chapter, is directly related to the intended use of the skate (see figure 2.2). Wheel size is measured in millimeters (mm). The diameter of a wheel is measured from one outer edge through the center of the wheel to the other outer edge. We have categorized wheel sizes by types of skating.

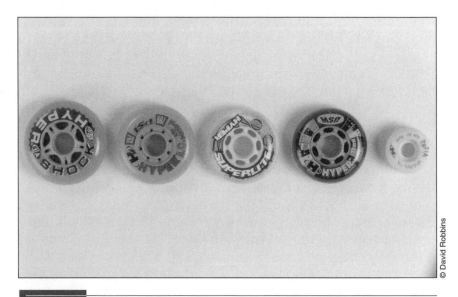

© David Robbins

FIGURE 2.2 Wheels come in all sizes. Which size you choose depends on the type of skating you'll do.

Recreational skate wheels.   Entry-level recreational skates are equipped with wheels that are 70 mm to 72 mm. These small wheels provide a lower center of gravity which allows the beginning skater to feel stable. Higher-grade recreational skates come with larger wheels (up to 80 mm) and allow faster skating. Larger wheels are generally for more advanced skaters.

Hockey wheels.   Most hockey players prefer a lower center of gravity and more security in turns, thus their wheels tend to be on the smaller side. The side of a hockey wheel tends to be more rounded than that of other wheels, for higher stability in a turn.

Fitness and cross-training wheels.   Midsize wheels are 72 mm to 76 mm, a good size for the skater who wants to skate longer distances for a good aerobic workout. This size is also common for indoor racing as it is more suitable for cornering than the larger outdoor racing wheel.

Aggressive/stunt wheels. This segment is perhaps the fastest-changing niche within the wheel market. Because a stunt skater wants to be as close to the ground as possible, small wheels (55 mm to 67 mm) are best for stunt skates. The profile of these wheels is very flat for higher stability. Wheels are made for street grinding, ramp leaping, and every niche within the stunt market. All of the wheels tend to be small and hard.

Race wheels. 78 mm to 82 mm wheels are the fastest, longest-lasting wheels because of their overall size and the inertia that their size and weight create. It takes more energy to get these wheels spinning, but, once in motion, they will continue to roll with less effort. The larger a wheel is, the more ground it covers with each rotation. Tall wheels are less stable side-to-side and, because of the additional height, they require a higher skill level. Race wheels also have the thinnest profile of all wheels for lighter weight. The thinner platform also contributes to increased speed and instability.

Urethane

Urethane is the hard rubber-like compound on the wheel that touches the ground. Urethane is a molded petroleum-based compound that can be made with different formulas to create wheels with varying degrees of hardness (durometer) and rebound.

Durometer. Durometer is a measurement of wheel hardness. This is the most common indicator of a wheel's skating and performance characteristics. Durometer of in-line wheels is measured by a two-digit number that indicates increasing hardness with increasing numbers. That is, a 78A wheel is softer than an 85A wheel. The letter A simply refers to the measurement scale that is used (A-scale). Current in-line wheels range from 75A to 93A with 78A and 82A being the most popular and versatile in the recreational market.

Intended use, skating surface, body weight, and skating abilities help determine which wheel is best to use (see table 2.1). A soft wheel has greater traction and cornering ability and will absorb more of the vibration from a rough skating

TABLE 2.1
DETERMINING WHICH WHEEL IS BEST TO USE

Skating surface	Body weight	Beginner	Intermediate	Advanced
Rough	Under 160 lb	78A	78A	78A
Rough	Over 160 lb	78A	78A	78A - 82A
Smooth pavement	Under 160 lb	78A	78A	78A
Smooth pavement	Over 160 lb	78A	78A	78A - 82A
Smooth concrete	Under 160 lb	78A	78A	78A
Smooth concrete	Over 160 lb	78A	82A-85A	82A - 85A
Indoor	Under 160 lb	85A	85A	85A
Indoor	Over 160 lb	85A	85A	85A

surface. A higher-durometer wheel will be faster and more efficient on a smooth skating surface, but on a rough road it will send vibrations through the skate and be very uncomfortable on your feet and legs.

Body weight of the skater also is important. A heavy skater will compress a soft wheel more and increase the footprint of the wheel, creating more drag and slowing the skater down. With that in mind, a heavier skater will want to skate on a harder wheel than a light skater.

Profile. The profile of a wheel refers to the shape of the urethane that surrounds the core (see figure 2.3). As noted earlier, various profiles can affect speed, cornering, and durability. A narrow-radius, pointed wheel has the least surface contact and therefore the least resistance. A wider-radius wheel has a larger footprint and is slower because of the greater resistance. However, the wider wheel is more stable and will last longer because of the additional urethane.

Rebound. The rebound of a wheel may be defined as the amount of energy put into the wheel that is returned, not absorbed into the energy source. In other words, low-rebound

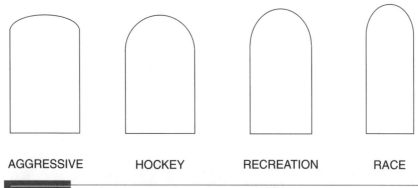

AGGRESSIVE   HOCKEY   RECREATION   RACE

FIGURE 2.3 Wheel profiles range from stubby for aggressive skating to pointy for racing.
Adapted, by permission, from Hyper Wheels. © Hyper, 1996.

wheels will make you work harder and feel like you're skating on a flat tire. A high-rebound wheel will go faster with less energy input and will feel more lively.

Rebound is not a characteristic that is defined by manufacturers on their wheels. The variations in rebound are a result of the type of urethane compound, or mix, that is used to make the wheel. In general, your local skate shop can direct you toward high-quality wheels that will have good rebound. The higher the rebound, the better.

Hub

At the center of the wheel, the hub separates the urethane from the bearings. Hubs are made of a stiff material that will not flex under the pressure of skating. The most common material used to make hubs is a thermoplastic nylon. In some specialty high-performance wheels, aluminum and carbon fiber are used.

In standard-size wheels, the hub may be just a thin sleeve in the center hole of the urethane that holds the bearings in place. In a large wheel, the hub may be up to 50 percent of the diameter and spoked (see figure 2.4). A well-designed spoked hub will help cool the urethane and bearings, maintain rigidity of the wheel, help tracking, and reduce overall weight.

Some inexpensive skates come with wheels that do not have hubs. This is another area where some manufacturers

© Hyper Wheels

FIGURE 2.4 A spoked hub will help cool a large wheel and keep it rigid.

cut back to reduce costs. These wheels do not roll as well as wheels with hubs.

Bearings

The term *bearings* refers to the ball bearings that allow the wheels of an in-line skate to spin smoothly. Modern bearings are sold in an enclosed doughnut-like metal casing that fits snugly into the center of a wheel's hub (see figure 2.5). Each wheel has two sets of bearings, one on each side of the wheel.

There are many different types and qualities of bearings, and it can be a difficult and time-consuming process to sort out all of the variables that affect bearing performance. In general, if you buy a quality pair of skates, you will get a quality set of bearings.

The rating system.   There is a bearings rating system that has become gospel in the skate industry today, but we feel it is misused and misunderstood by skate manufacturers, retail

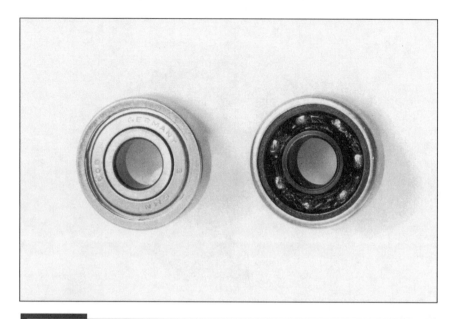

FIGURE 2.5 The closed-casing bearing set on the left is what modern bearings look like. With the cover removed on the right you can see the bearings inside the case.

stores, and ultimately consumers. Skate bearings are now sold based on the following ratings system: precision, semi-precision, ABEC-1, ABEC-3, and ABEC-5. This system, as determined by the American Bearing Engineering Committee, refers to the tolerance of the inner and outer races and of the bearing balls, and the noise level measured in decibels. Tolerances of the races and the balls refer to how precisely the bearings and the races (or channels) that encase them are ground. In other words, the smaller the tolerance, the closer to perfectly round the ball bearings are and the closer to perfectly circular the races are.

But there are many other issues that are more important in rating bearings. Carbon steel balls are significantly less expensive—and less durable—than stainless steel balls. The type of grease used to pack the bearings will have a tremendous effect on both the cost and the life of the bearings. A good grease will pack out the edges of the bearing shield and protect the inner workings of the bearings from the intrusion of dirt and grit. Some bearings use very light oils, and the spin of the wheels when you take the skate off the store shelf is great. However, these oils quickly dry out or vacate the inner housing of the bearing, causing the bearing to wear out very quickly. Cheaper bearings do not have C-rings that will allow you to remove the outer shields and maintain your bearings.

Rather than depending on the ratings system, which means very little, we advise that you not base your buying decisions on the rating of the bearings. Instead, ask the following questions:

- What type of lubricant is used?
- Do the bearings have C-rings?
- Is the price reasonable?

In this case, it tends to be true that you get what you pay for.

Rocker

Rocker refers to a position of the wheels on your in-line skates in which they do not all rest flat on the ground at once. For example, on a four-wheel skate, the center two wheels are adjusted to be taller, so that when standing on a flat surface the front and back wheels will be off the ground approximately 1/8th of an inch.

Setting your skates on a rocker will allow you to turn and spin faster than leaving them on a flat plane, but this can cause instability when traveling at higher speeds or over long distances. Advanced skaters commonly set their wheels on a rocker for hockey or tricks and dance skating.

To set the wheels in the rocker position, remove the center two wheels (just the middle wheel on three-wheel skates). You will see frame spacers inserted in a hole in the frame. The spacers have a hole that the axle passes through. Some spacers offer two positions for adjustment and are oblong, like Rollerblade spacers. Other spacers, like K2, are hexagonal and offer a greater range of positions. Pop the spacers out and turn them over so the axle hole is toward the bottom of the frame. You can then reinstall the center wheels.

You can also shorten the wheel base through the same process. Remove the front and back wheel and you will see that there are spacers that allow you to adjust the length of the wheel base. A longer wheel base is faster and more stable. A shorter wheel base helps you turn and spin faster.

Although these adjustments cause changes of only a fraction of an inch in the wheel base, you will be amazed at how unstable the skates feel. You should attempt skating on short, rockered skates only when you feel comfortable and confident on a flat skate. Even then, it will take a considerable amount of time to feel comfortable on rockered skates, but the performance benefits for dance, trick, and hockey skating are great.

TYPES OF IN-LINE SKATES

As the sport of in-line skating continues to grow, more types of skates appear on the market. In this section, we will examine the various types of skates currently available.

INEXPENSIVE SKATES

The market is flooded with in-line skates selling for less than $100. These prices are meant to capitalize on the popularity and trendiness of the new sport. They do fill a niche in the market, but they cannot be considered serious sporting equipment. These skates utilize only hard-shell technology.

The manufacturers of these types of skates save money by using inexpensive plastics in the boot and frame. This plastic does not give the same ankle support as a higher-quality skate. Remember, ankle support is one of the keys to being able to skate comfortably and safely.

In addition, most of these skates have very low-grade bearings and no hubs in the wheels. As a result, the skates do not roll well. It can be very frustrating to stroke and stroke and not roll at all.

Skates that retail for less than $100 may be a good option for children who are still growing and want an introduction to in-line skating (see figure 2.6). But adults who desire any amount of aerobic or serious recreational workout should avoid inexpensive skates.

© David Robbins

| FIGURE 2.6 | Most children's skates are available for under $100. |

The investment that you make in a quality pair of skates will pay for itself many times over when compared to many other sports or membership in a health club. As an additional bonus, quality used skates maintain a tremendously high resale value.

RECREATIONAL SKATES

The majority of skates sold today are recreational skates. Recreational skates provide the versatility to skate in many different fashions. Don't be fooled by the word *recreation*— these skates can be used for everything from aerobic workouts to hockey.

The reverse is also true: That is, any good skates, whatever their label (fitness and cross-training, hockey, racing, etc.), are fine for recreational skating as long as they provide good ankle support with quality wheels and bearings (see figure 2.7) and you feel comfortable skating in them. Official recreation skates

Courtesy of K2

FIGURE 2.7 Good adult recreational skates sell for $125 to $300.

can range in price from approximately $125 to $300. Finding the best pair of skates for your budget and needs is a matter of testing various skates and shopping for the best price and service combination.

FITNESS AND CROSS-TRAINING SKATES

Fitness and cross-training skates (see figure 2.8) are used by athletes who are trying to emulate the Nordic skiing stride (or some other cross-training activity) or are simply looking for a great workout on a pair of skates. These skates tend to have lower cuffs than recreational skates and, in many cases, a longer wheel base.

Additionally, these skates tend to have larger wheels for more speed as well as better, faster bearings. Expect to pay over $200 for a pair of quality fitness or cross-training skates. You can pay up to $400 for a really high-end pair.

Courtesy of K2

FIGURE 2.8   Fitness and cross-training skate.

STUNT SKATES

Stunt skating is perhaps the fastest-growing and fastest-changing niche within in-line skating. Stunt skates (see figure 2.9) are built extremely low to the ground and have many add-on accessories such as grind plates, which let the user grind on curbs and do rail slides (literally sliding down a railing with your skates). Always four-wheel skates, better stunt skates do not have uniform spacing among the four wheels. Instead, there is additional space between the center two wheels for rail slides. Better stunt skates will also have metal buckles and generally are built to withstand grinding on all surfaces. Please note that high-end stunt skates do not come with brakes, and most manufacturers do not offer brakes for them. Therefore, you must be able to do the T-stop or Y-stop (you will learn how to execute them in chapter 6). Hockey stops, which are very difficult for all but the best skaters and

Courtesy of K2

FIGURE 2.9   Stunt skate.

require a perfect skating surface, are not used—unless you want to fall!

RACE SKATES

Race skates (see figure 2.10) are used not only for racing but for long-distance skating. They are typically component-driven; that is, you build the skates by putting together a series of components. The components comprising a race skate are the boot, the frame, the hardware (axles and spacers), and the wheels. Like stunt and hockey skates, the best race skates have no brakes. These skates have several differences from other types of in-line skates. The most obvious differences are a frame length of 13 inches to 15 inches and one extra wheel. The longer frame provides a more stable and directed stroke and glide but restricts the turning radius of the skater. It is important that the frame be made of a very

© David Robbins

FIGURE 2.10   Race skate.

stiff but lightweight material such as a composite or a metal alloy.

Although race skates usually have five wheels, occasionally they will have only four if the skater has small feet or wants to reduce the weight of the skates. The wheels on racing skates are usually larger in diameter than those on other skates, 76 mm to 82 mm. A larger wheel has greater surface area, so it rotates fewer times per mile.

The combination of a longer frame and more and larger wheels offers both disadvantages and advantages. The main disadvantage is increased weight, which can take its toll on a racer's or distance skater's performance. Manufacturers combat this problem by using high-tech, lightweight components such as 100 percent carbon frames, but these also drive prices up. Most component boots and frames come with hardware that lets the consumer attach the frame to the boot very easily. If not, it is best to work with a shop that you trust.

The longer frame is more difficult to push out and away from your body during a stroke. Therefore, acceleration and climbing hills tends to be slower on a long frame. The real advantage of these skates becomes apparent once you get them up to a pace or racing speed. The stability and inertia of a long frame and large wheels will have a significant positive effect on your ability to maintain a high speed with the least amount of effort.

You will also find differences in a race boot from other skates. The race boot is cut lower around the ankle and preferably constructed of a lightweight yet stiff material. These boots are filled with a heat-moldable thermoplastic material and must be molded to your feet in order to be worn comfortably. In many cases, top racers use the same leather boots that ice speed skaters use. This is not ideal, as the tender leather of such a boot is no match for asphalt in a fall. A few manufacturers are just now addressing this issue by building low-cut, high-end, heat-moldable race boots with tougher exterior coverings.

A quality pair of in-line race skates will cost between $350 and $600. Most skaters will find that skates in the $400 price range will meet their needs. Anticipate spending slightly more money each year on wheels and bearings than for recreational skates. More miles skated equals more frequent replacement of wheels and bearings.

DANCE SKATES

In recent years, dance skating has broken away from stunt skating as a category. One manufacturer, Risport, makes in-line skates that emulate the feel of figure skating, but it is difficult to find the skates in the United States. In most cases, athletes who prefer to dance on skates use a high-end pair of recreational skates. As stunt skating has soared in popularity, little has been done to service the small dance skating niche.

Now that the United States Amateur Confederation of Roller Skating has decided to allow in-line skates into their competitions, it will be interesting to see what kind of impact the in-line skaters have on the artistic competitions.

If you want to dance on in-line skates, there are some key features you should look for in skates. They should have a very stiff boot and frame. Because of the types of turns and jumps you may be doing, you will put a lot of lateral (sideways) pressure on the skates. If the skate is constructed of lightweight material, it will flex under this pressure. If the boot flexes, you'll lose ankle support, and if the frame bends, you'll lose control.

Smaller diameter wheels are also important on dance skates. They will help lower your center of gravity and make you more stable. The hardness of wheels you should choose will vary depending on the skating surface. Use a harder wheel on a smooth surface and a softer wheel on a rough surface.

It is also important to buy skates that have frames that allow you to rocker the wheels. Although you may not rocker the wheels right away, you'll want to have that option available as your skill level increases (for more information on rockering, see the section in Components of In-Line Skates, page 29).

HOCKEY SKATES

In-line hockey (also called roller hockey), like stunt skating, has soared in popularity in recent years. Many in-line skate manufacturers are now offering skates specifically designed for roller hockey (see figure 2.11). These skates have a relatively short frame and the option of rockering the wheels, allowing the skater to turn and spin quickly. The boot and frame of the skates are built with heavier plastics so they will stand up to the abuses of hockey.

Some manufacturers have simply taken their ice hockey boots and mounted them on in-line frames for street use. This is not ideal. The fabrics on the uppers of ice hockey boots shred quickly after asphalt abrasion. The best boots for in-line hockey feature no fabric over the toe bump area and strategically placed plastic to protect the upper from street wear.

There are now wheels specifically designed for hockey players as well. Most hockey wheels are small (70 mm to 72 mm in diameter) and lower the skater's center of gravity. As street

Courtesy of K2

FIGURE 2.11 Hockey skate.

hockey players' skills improve, the current trend favors larger wheels for more speed. These also have a very wide profile so the skates can be turned sharply without sliding out from under the skater. Wheel manufacturers are now making different wheels for indoor and outdoor hockey use.

SKATE MAINTENANCE

In-line skates are relatively low-maintenance, and that is one of the inviting aspects of the sport. You can put on your skates and get a good workout without a lot of setup or cleanup time. However, your skates will need attention from time to time.

It's a great idea to put together a skate repair kit that you can carry in your skate bag. A list of recommended tools ap-

TABLE 2.2

RECOMMENDED TOOLS FOR MAINTENANCE

Minimum requirements	Suggested additions
2 Allen wrenches	Bearings
1 box wrench or socket wrench (socket preferred)	Washers (if used on your axles)
	Spare axle
1 bearing removal tool	Replacement brake
1 screwdriver (for brake replacement; check for Phillips or regular)	Spare wheels
	Frame spacers
Cleaning rags	Bearing spacers
Sharp pin or needle	Extra laces
Paint thinner or solvent	Toothbrush
2 small bowls	Paper towels
Bearing gel	Cotton swabs

pears in table 2.2. Be sure to choose components and tools that fit your particular model of skates—different skates have different sizes of wheels, wrenches, and so forth. Your local skate shop can help you with the selection of components and tools.

BEARING MAINTENANCE

Bearings do wear out with use. One indication of wear is a grinding noise coming from the bearing when the wheel is spinning. This noise is the result of a breakdown of the grease that the bearings are packed in, or of sand, rust particles, or some other foreign material getting into the bearing casing.

It is possible to take the bearing casing apart (see figure 2.12), clean the bearings, repack the case with grease, and replace the casing cover (the shield). Buying a new set of bearings is not costly and is much easier than rebuilding an old set. Some manufacturers, such as Twin Cam, have programs

Bearing Weardown and Maintenance

There are a number of reasons why bearings wear out, but if you are aware of the signs and you use proper care and maintenance, you can keep your bearings in good running order. Refer to figure 2.12 on page 42, which shows the different parts of the bearing. The five most common reasons for bearing weardown are:

1. **Contamination of the lubricant.** This is the most common reason for bearing failure.

   Signs: Dents or scratches on the balls and materials embedded in the raceway.

   Causes: Conditions of the skating surface, dirty tools or hands.

   Action: Clean and relubricate the bearings.

   Prevention: Avoid skating on wet surfaces or surfaces with a lot of dirt, sand, or gravel. Always be sure to have clean hands and clean tools when working on skates.

2. **Lubricant failure.** This can cause excessive wear on the bearings, eventually causing them to lock up and stop spinning altogether.

   Signs: Blue or brown ball tracks left behind when skating.

   Causes: Choosing the wrong type of lubricant for the specific condition or use, which may restrict the flow of the lubricant. Oil-packed bearings are not recommended as they are more prone to water washout and lubricant leakage.

   Action: Relubricate bearings with a more protective gel recommended by your in-line skating dealer.

   Prevention: Use a thicker, more protective gel.

3. **Improper assembly of the bearings.** A loose fit can cause wear, heat, noise, and lubricant runout. A tight fit will cause an increase in temperature and in torque, resulting in bearing failure.

Signs: *Loose fit*—Wear or discoloration of the outer and inner mounting surface of the bearings.

Tight fit—Heavy ball-wear paths at the bottom of the raceway.

Causes: *Loose fit*—The bearing and its mating parts have been fitted too loosely.

Tight fit—The bearing's radial clearance has been distorted by being fitted too tightly.

Action: Remove the bearings from the skate and reassemble.

Prevention: Use the proper tools and the proper torque for the mounting bolts.

4. **Misalignment of the bearings.** This can cause an increase in operating temperature, which will result in heavy wear and bearing failure.

Signs: A skewed ball-wear path.

Causes: Incorrect installation.

Action: Remove the bearings from the skate and reassemble.

Prevention: Be sure to follow all instructions properly when installing your bearings and to check your work.

5. **Exposure to corrosive materials.** This can cause an increase in vibration, which will result in excess wear of the bearings.

Signs: Red or brown staining of balls, raceways, cages, or bands.

Causes: Exposure to a corrosive fluid or atmosphere.

Action: Take off bearings and completely relubricate.

Prevention: Though this is not a common problem, be careful to keep away from corrosive fluids or areas where they are being used.

Adapted by permission from TWINCAM in-line bearing™.

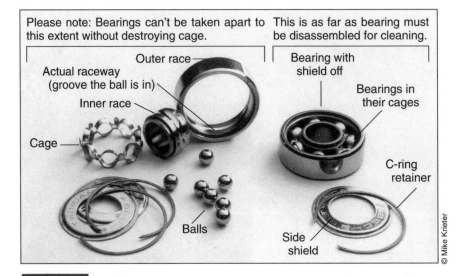

Please note: Bearings can't be taken apart to this extent without destroying cage. This is as far as bearing must be disassembled for cleaning.

Outer race
Actual raceway (groove the ball is in)
Inner race
Cage
Balls
Bearing with shield off
Bearings in their cages
C-ring retainer
Side shield
© Mike Krieter

FIGURE 2.12   Bearings fully seperated.

that allow you to send back your bearings so they may re-build them for a nominal fee. Consult your local skate shop for options on replacement bearings.

A set of bearings should last a year if you take care of them and avoid moisture, sand, and heavy dust. The outer bearing casings attract a lot of dust, so wipe them clean on a regular basis.

BEARING CLEANING AND RELUBRICATION

Before you start, you will need the following from your tool kit: sharp pin or needle, bearing removal tool, toothbrush, paint thinner or solvent, clean rags, paper towels, cotton swabs, two clean bowls, and the appropriate bearing gel. Then follow these steps:

1. Remove wheels as noted on pages 48-50. Wipe off any loose sand or dirt. Place bolts from the wheels in one of the bowls.

2. Locate the retaining C-ring on the front surface and find the end that points toward the center of the bearing. Place the end of the pin or needle under the pointed edge of the C-ring and carefully push toward the center of the bearing with an upward and outward motion. This will free one side. Then simply remove the C-ring by hand and place it in the bowl with the bolts. Repeat this process for the other wheels.

3. Place the bearing removal tool into the axle hole and press the bearing on the opposite side of the wheel out of the wheel hub (see figure 2.13). Turn the wheel over and remove the nylon or aluminum bearing spacer (see figure 2.14). (The bearing spacer provides a lining for the axle to pass through and keeps the bearings from sliding into the center of the hub.) Keep the spacers with the C-rings.

4. Put the bearing removal tool through the hub from the back side and press the second bearing out. Place all the bearings in the empty bowl.

5. With a damp cloth, remove all dirt and grime from the inside of the wheel hub. If the inside of the bearing spacers is dirty, use a cotton swab to remove the dirt. If the bearing spacers show wear, replace them with new ones.

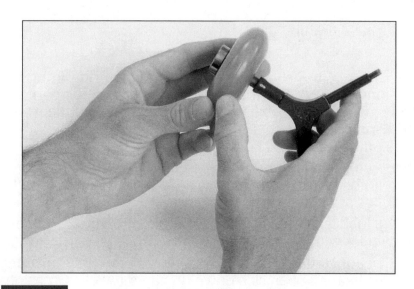

FIGURE 2.13 Use a bearing removal tool to press the bearings out of the wheel hub.

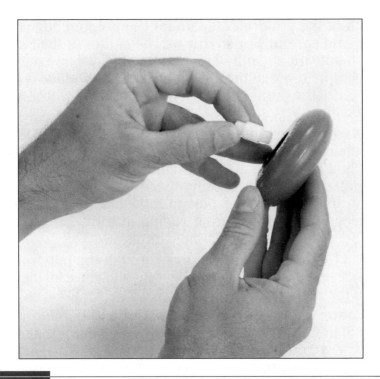

FIGURE 2.14 Turn the wheel over, remove the bearing spacer, and press the second bearing out from the back side of the bearing.

6. Most of the shields should have fallen off during the cleaning process, but if not, simply tap the bearing on the table to free them. Wipe the shields clean and put them with the C-rings and spacers.

7. Rinse bearings with paint thinner and repeat several times with clean thinner. Be sure to work in a well-ventilated area. If the bearings are heavily soiled, rinse only half of the bearings at a time.

8. If lubricant remains on the bearings after rinsing, remove remainder with a toothbrush. Repeat process as necessary.

9. Bearings must be completely dry before relubricating. Lay the bearing open side down on paper towels. Occasionally turn the bearings to speed up the process, or you may even use a hair dryer set on the lowest setting.

10. Once the bearings are completely dry, relubricate with an appropriate gel for your skating needs. Squeeze a thin bead of lubricant over the ball bearing surface.

11. Replace the shields on the open bearings with retaining C-rings. To reinstall the C-rings, take both ends and gently squeeze them together, slide the round end under the retaining lip of the bearing, release the ends, and push under the retaining lip. Use a pin to ensure that the entire C-ring is securely fitted.

12. Reassemble the bearings and inner spacers onto the wheels.

13. Replace the wheels according to the instructions given on pages 48-50.

14. Slowly spin the wheels to work the new gel into the bearings before skating. There may be some leakage. If so, simply wipe clean.

BEARING REPLACEMENT

To replace the bearings, first follow steps 1 and 3–5 on pages 42–43, then:

● Insert a new bearing casing into one side of the wheel hub. Be sure to press the bearing case into the hub until it is flush with the edge of the hub. Turn the wheel over and insert the bearing spacer. Align the second bearing case with the spacer and press it into the hub. Be careful to align properly so as not to press the side of the bearing casing into the ball bearings with the end of the spacer.

● Replace the wheels according to the instructions given on pages 48-50, then follow these directions:

If you are installing new wheels, follow the same instructions, but insert your current bearings into the new wheels.

WHEEL ROTATION OR REPLACEMENT

Wheels wear down while skating. To get the maximum mileage, proper rotation (changing the wheel's position on the frame and turning the wheels over so the inside edge becomes the outside edge) is necessary. While rotation is the most common maintenance task you will perform on your skates, sometimes the wheels are so worn you must replace them altogether.

When to Rotate

Take a good look at your wheels to see the wear patterns (see figure 2.15). If the wheels are starting to look worn at an angle along the inside edges, it's time to rotate them. Most commonly the inside edges of the wheels wear down more quickly than the outside due to the sideways pushing motion of skating. Wheels may also be worn down more in the front or in the rear, depending on whether you push off with your toe or your heel. Every skater strokes differently, so everyone creates a unique wear pattern on their wheels.

Order of Rotation

We will refer to the front wheel as position number one, the second wheel as position number two, and so on (see figure 2.16).

To rotate your wheels, follow these directions:

Wheel in position:	Move to position:	
1	to	3
2	to	4
3	to	1
4	to	2

You will notice that you are moving the front and back wheels to the center positions. With three- and five-wheel skates, move the most worn wheels to the position of the wheels that show the least amount of wear. To take the wheels off and put them back on, follow the directions in Wheel Rotation and Replacement.

If you are using skates that have a protruding nut (as opposed to flush-mounted hardware), you will notice that the axle bolts opposite the nuts have a flush head. It is imperative that the flush heads face the inside of the skate (see

46

FIGURE 2.15 On the left is a new wheel. On the right is a wheel that's heavily worn; it should have been rotated before the wear became so extreme.

Courtesy of K2

FIGURE 2.16 The labels show the pattern for rotating wheels.

47

figure 2.17). As you push your skate out when stroking, the inside edge of the frame comes close to the ground. If you replace the axle bolt with the nut end on the inside, it is relatively easy to hit the bolt when stroking. This can be very dangerous as the bolt and nut may catch on the ground or slide out from under you when the metal contacts the ground.

Wheel Rotation and Replacement

Knowing when your wheels should be replaced is a judgment call. When wheels get too small or worn down, they are less functional and can be less safe as well. For example, the wheels can be worn so far down that when you take a corner, the frame will scrape the pavement, causing you to fall. Also, a worn wheel means less urethane between you and

© Lesley Ellam

FIGURE 2.17 This skater's left skate would catch on the axle bolts if they weren't flush with the frame.

the pavement and therefore a rougher ride. Pay attention to these factors and make your own decision.

To remove and replace or rotate the wheels, follow these steps:

1. Brace the skate between your legs with the wheels up (see figure 2.18). Using the appropriate wrenches, loosen and remove each axle.

2. Rotate the wheels to the appropriate position or replace with new wheels. If you are rotating them, wipe all dust and grime from the bearing casing and the frame spacers. Remember to flip the wheels so the worn side is now facing out. (There is no need to rotate wheels from one skate to the other unless you have a dramatic wear difference between skates.)

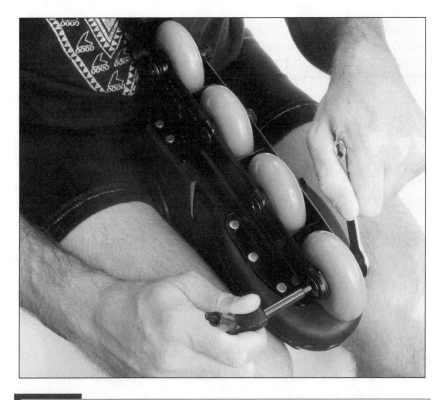

FIGURE 2.18 Position and tools for wheel rotation and replacement.

3. Realign the wheels with the axle holes, insert the axle bolt, and screw the nut on (nut facing the outside edge of the frame). Tighten each axle and nut until snug.

4. Spin each wheel to make sure it spins freely. If a wheel does not spin well, loosen the axle nut slightly and try to spin it again. If you have a wheel that makes noise when it spins, it may be time to replace the bearings. Attempt to identify which bearing is making the noise and replace it (see Bearing Replacement on page 45).

It should be noted that the axle bolt for the wheel closest to the brake is longer than the other axle bolts. The part of the frame that holds the brake in place is secured with the back axle. Be sure to replace this bolt in its original position.

BRAKE REPLACEMENT

Brakes wear out and should be replaced when you have to lift your toe too high to be stable when stopping or when the bolt holding the brake in place begins to rub the ground. Your local skate shop can provide you with a replacement brake for your model of skates.

Brakes have a through bolt that can be loosened with either a screwdriver, Allen wrench, or socket wrench, depending on the type of brake you have. The replacement of the brake is straightforward. Simply loosen the bolt, remove the brake, and attach the new brake (see figure 2.19).

UPGRADING YOUR SKATES

If you have previously purchased a pair of inexpensive in-line skates and have decided that the performance is unsatisfactory, you do not have to start from scratch with a brand-new pair of skates. Most of the important components on your skates can be upgraded for less money than buying a new pair of skates.

The first item to consider replacing is bearings. Bearings can have the most negative effect on the performance of inexpensive skates. Check with your local skate shop for a quality

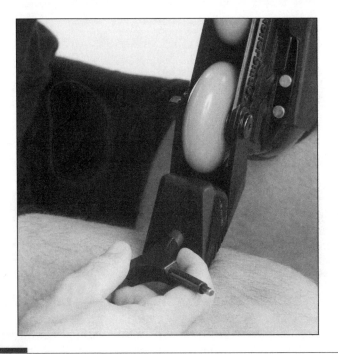

FIGURE 2.19 Different brakes have different systems for securing them. Most are easily replaced.

set of bearings. You do not have to buy a high-performance set of bearings to see an increase in performance.

While at the skate shop, check into upgrading your wheels. Refer to the section on wheels in this chapter and consult with experts at the shop about the type of wheels you should select. Bearings and wheels can be purchased at separate times. If cash flow is a consideration, get the bearings first.

SAFETY GEAR

This section on safety gear could be the most important part of this book. Safety is crucial for in-line skaters. Take the time and money to invest in the appropriate safety gear (see figure 2.20) and use it.

FIGURE 2.20   It's important to wear the full range of safety gear.

TO USE OR NOT TO USE

When skating, and when looking at the pictures in this book, you will see some skaters without appropriate safety gear. An experienced skater skating without safety gear is taking a calculated risk based on her skills and the skating conditions.

For example, it would be unusual to see bicycle racers with knee pads on, but they always wear helmets. They have decided to risk scrapes and bruises because the knee pads can interfere with their performance, but not to risk a skull fracture. The same is true for racers on in-line skates. They all wear helmets, but the number who wear knee pads and elbow pads is relatively small. This personal decision is one of skills versus risks.

It would be a foolish decision for an inexperienced skater to practice or learn to skate without wearing appropriate safety gear.

THE GEAR

With that in mind, here is a list of suggested safety gear:

1. Helmet—Few helmets are made specifically for in-line skating. Check the selection at your local bike shop. Select a helmet that is Snell safety certified and provides a snug, comfortable fit.

2. Wrist guards—The most common injuries from skating accidents are sprained or broken wrists. This is a result of the skater putting out a hand and arm to break a fall. It does not take much speed to injure a wrist. Wear wrist guards at all times! The plastic brace is worn on the inside of the wrist so it crosses the palm of the hand (see figure 2.21). As with gloves,

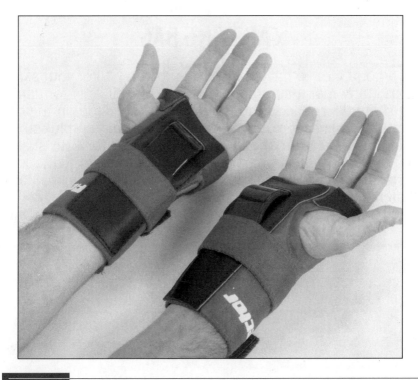

FIGURE 2.21 Wrist guards. The plastic bar should cover the bottom of the wrist and palm of the hand.

wrist guards are made for the right and left hands. They are not interchangeable.

3. Knee pads and elbow pads—Knee pads and elbow pads are designed to help avoid scrapes and bruises. Use only the style with a hard plastic shield over the pad. Do not use cloth-covered pads from other sports such as volleyball. If you fall, these pads will not slide across the cement or asphalt. Instead, they catch and then slide up the leg or arm, exposing the joint that should be protected. The plastic-covered pads slide across the surface upon contact.

The money you spend on safety gear is a wise investment. If you can't afford safety gear, you can't afford to skate! (For additional information on extra safety gear for roller hockey, see chapter 11.)

CARRYING BAG

It's a good idea to have a large bag to carry all of your skate gear. Many manufacturers make bags specifically for carrying skate gear. Check with your local skate shop on the options. Another spot to check is an Army or Navy surplus store. Look for a bag with one large compartment for your skates and several smaller compartments for your safety gear, tools, parts, and some extra skate clothes, including socks. Many skaters like to carry their complete skating bag in their car so they can take advantage of any available time to go skating.

GETTING STARTED

Before you start in-line skating, it is important to take a few more things into consideration. In this chapter we will look at some important pre-skate activities.

Remember that in-line skating is a strenuous activity. If your physical health is questionable in any way, consult your doctor before starting to in-line skate. Once you've settled that issue, you can go on to other pre-skating matters you should think about.

RULES OF THE ROAD

When in-line skating was in its infancy, the International In-Line Skating Association (IISA) had the foresight to develop Rules of the Road as a guide for skaters. The rules are still excellent for all skaters to follow. Here they are:

1. Wear safety equipment: wrist guards, knee and elbow pads, and a helmet.
2. Stay alert and be courteous at all times.
3. Control your speed.
4. Skate on the right side of paths, trails, and sidewalks.
5. Overtake other pedestrians, cyclists, and skaters on the left. Use extra caution and announce your intentions by saying, "Passing on your left." Pass only when it is safe, and when you both have enough room for the full extension position of your stroke.
6. Be aware of changes in trail conditions due to traffic, weather conditions, and hazards such as water, potholes, or storm debris. When in doubt, slow down. Do not skate on wet or oily surfaces.
7. Obey all traffic regulations. When on skates, you have the same obligations as a moving vehicle.
8. Stay out of areas with heavy automobile traffic.
9. Always yield to pedestrians.
10. Before using any trail, achieve a basic skill level, including the ability to turn, control speed, brake going down hills, and recognize and avoid skating obstacles.

KEEPING IN-LINE SKATING LEGAL

In-line skating's phenomenal growth has led to a dramatic increase in the number of skaters all across the United States. Because of this increase and the perception of danger by the nonskating public, many cities regulate or even forbid skaters access to public parks, trails, and roads.

Although the IISA has successfully fought against these regulations in many cities, legal issues surrounding in-line skating will be debated for a long time to come. One of the most effective ways you can minimize legal challenges to in-line skating in your community is to promote a positive image of skaters. The IISA Government Relations Committee has recommended the following 10 ways to do this:

1. Skate smart. Build the image of the in-line skater as a safety-conscious individual.
2. Align with the bicyclist. Bikers enjoy the type of access skaters need, and few consider them a bother. Let their image rub off on you.
3. Sponsor family days. People respond positively to seeing families interact in activity settings, and in-line skating is a great family activity.
4. Skate with community leaders. Many would love to learn how to in-line skate. Why not volunteer to educate them?
5. Offer your help to the law enforcement community. Check with your police department to see whether they have a civilian patrol or any other program that could use you on skates.
6. Teach safety clinics. Contact your local park district, community center, or YMCA; they might sponsor the event and let you use their facilities.
7. Attend regulatory meetings (traffic, city, school). Wear your nice clothes and present a professional image.
8. Present a school program. Get educators behind the in-line movement.
9. Visit the rental shop. Advertise safety clinics there and leave flyers with safety tips for customers.

10. Police yourself. Remember that in-line skating is very cool, very fun, and can be quite wacky, but as a role model for the beginner, you should execute your stranger and more dangerous maneuvers out of public view. By all means push the sport and make the most of your skate, but also skate smart, skate polite, and, when appropriate, skate stealth!

Adapted by permission from the IISA.

WHERE TO SKATE

Fortunately, you can in-line skate in a number of outdoor or in-door locations. Two factors will determine the best location for you: the type of skating that interests you and your skill level.

OUTSIDE

If you are a beginner who is still learning the fundamentals of in-line skating, look for a large, smooth, flat surface with as few obstructions as possible. Two good locations are the blacktop of a school yard or a large, paved parking lot. Choose either of these options only when they are not being used, and always obey no-trespassing rules.

As your skill level increases, look for similar wide-open surfaces but with a slight downhill grade so you can practice connecting turns while coasting downhill (you'll learn about connecting turns in chapter 7).

When you reach a proficient skill level in stroking, turning, stopping, and avoiding obstacles, your skating opportunities open up greatly. Traditional bicycle trails are a great place to get a scenic long-distance workout. To learn more about trail systems, contact your local park district and ask if they publish a map of trails.

If you have a large bicycling community in your city, check with a local bike shop and find out if any criterium bike racing goes on in the area. If so, find out the locations and times of their races and practices. Criterium bike racing is similar to in-line skate racing, and their training grounds may be a good training area for in-line skating, too.

Wherever you decide to skate, obey the rules of the road, skate smart, and respect the rights of private property owners. You and those you skate with have the responsibility to keep skating safe and legal in your community.

INSIDE

The most obvious place to in-line skate indoors is the roller skating rink. Many roller rink operators around the United States were originally hesitant to allow in-line skaters to use their rinks. They were afraid that wood floors in the rink might be scratched by in-line skates and that in-line skating would displace roller skating. But as the popularity of in-line skating grew, the rink operators realized that their fears were unfounded and that opening up to in-line skaters could only help business. Today, most roller rinks allow in-line skates and many offer in-line skates as rentals.

STRETCHING

Before you put your skates on, it is important to spend time stretching and warming up. Investing 15 minutes preparing your body for a workout will go a long way toward reducing your risk of injury. Warming up will also help you feel more relaxed and confident as you skate.

Begin your pre-skate activities by walking, jogging, or even skating slowly for 5 to 10 minutes for a gradual warm-up. The object is to get your blood circulating throughout your muscles *before* you begin stretching them. Once you have warmed up, you can begin the stretches outlined on pages 60–63.

These eight stretching exercises will help loosen and warm up the primary muscle groups that are used while in-line skating. It is important to execute each stretch slowly, without bouncing or jerking the muscle. Stretch to the point of slight discomfort, not pain, and hold for 20 to 30 seconds. It takes at least this long to properly stretch any muscle.

Proper breathing during the stretches is important to help increase your lung capacity and assist in being loose and relaxed. While doing each stretch, relax the rest of your body and exhale slowly on the exertion phase.

Neck Drop your head forward until your chin touches your chest; hold for 20 seconds. Drop your head back; hold for 20 seconds. Tilt your head toward your shoulder and hold for 20 seconds, once each side. In order to increase the stretch, you may add slight pressure by gently pulling your neck with your hand as shown.

Quadriceps Stand facing a wall or flat surface with one hand against it for balance. Bend one leg at the knee and raise your foot up behind the buttocks. Hold the raised foot with your free hand and pull the foot toward the buttocks. Hold the stretch for 20 seconds. Stretch both legs.

Back and Hamstrings Sit on the ground with one leg out straight and bend the other leg at the knee, resting the sole against the inner thigh of the straight leg. Bend forward at the waist and grasp the foot of the straight leg. Hold the stretch for 20 seconds. Stretch both legs.

Buttocks and Hips Sit on the ground with one leg extended and cross the other leg over, placing the foot flat on the ground near the knee. Twist the upper body in the direction of the bent leg and balance on one hand. Place the other arm on the outside of the raised knee, applying pressure to the knee. Hold the stretch for 20 seconds. Stretch both legs.

Groin Sit on the ground with both legs extended and spread apart as far as comfortably possible. Lean forward at the waist and lower the upper body over one leg. Hold the stretch for 20 seconds. Stretch both legs.

Ankle and Calf Sit on the ground with one leg out straight and cross the other leg over, resting the ankle on the top of the knee of the straight leg. Hold the crossover leg at the top of the foot. Pull the foot toward your body. Hold the stretch for 20 seconds. Stretch both legs.

Low Back Lie on your back and raise your knees. Bending at the waist, grab your knees and bring them up to your chest. Leave your head flat against the ground. Hold the stretch for 20 seconds.

SKATING FUNDAMENTALS

You may be learning to in-line skate purely for fun and exercise, or you may want to learn to race, skate aggressively (street or vertical), or play roller hockey. Whatever your reason for taking up skating, the fundamentals are the foundation on which you will build.

It's not difficult to go out, put on in-line skates and safety gear, and take a few laps around a park. But just as in skiing and many other sports, the trial and error method is not the smartest way to learn. Your learning curve will be substantially slower and the risk of injury greater than with good instruction. In addition, it's difficult to analyze and correct your own mistakes without some knowledge.

Stopping is the most common concern among new in-line skaters. However, before you read the chapter on stopping, it is important that you have a good understanding of the posture and balance skills you need. To help build your solid foundation of skating skills, please read the chapters in the order presented here.

The material in this part will analyze the basics of in-line skating: posture, stroke and glide, stopping, turns, and then putting it all together. You will learn the proper execution of each basic skill and you will also see the common mistakes that people make. This knowledge will help you see and understand the subtle difference between the right way and the wrong way to build your foundation.

As much as this book will help you, nothing will replace practice and time on your skates. Take time to study the following chapters, then give yourself time to practice and learn. Wear your safety gear and follow the rules of the road. Skate smart!

CHAPTER 4

POSTURE AND BALANCE

© Kenneth Redding

Proper posture is the most important element of good in-line skating fundamentals. Most beginning skaters fall because their skates zoom out in front of them as they fall backward. Not a very exciting introduction to an exciting sport! Without exception, these falls can be attributed to improper posture.

Skill Checklist

To be sure you're applying the lessons we are about to teach you, read this chapter carefully and practice the drills until you feel comfortable doing them. Then go over the following checklist in your mind every time you skate until these techniques become second nature:

1. Keep your weight forward over the balls of your feet.

2. Swing hands side-to-side in front of your body.

3. Relax and keep your knees bent so they can act as shock absorbers.

ELEMENTS OF POSTURE

Posture is the positioning of your body, arms, hands, legs, and skates so they are balanced and centered. If your posture is good, your body will stay centered over your skates even while your skating environment, conditions, and speeds change.

As previously stated, the most common fall on in-line skates occurs when your body weight is too far back and the skates zoom out in front of you, causing you to fall backward. You can avoid this kind of fall with proper posture and weight distribution.

68

HAND POSITION

The most common error that skaters of all skill levels make is allowing their hands to swing behind their hips. It's very natural to swing your hands front-to-back when walking or running, and most people do the same thing when skating, but it is very dangerous.

As your hand swings back behind your hip, it pulls your shoulder and upper-body weight back onto your heel. You then become unstable and your skates get out ahead of you. If the skates get out in front a little too far, boom—you're on the ground!

It's natural to swing your arms and hands when skating: The key is to swing them left-to-right, across the front of your body (see figure 4.1), never allowing your hands to swing behind your hips.

FIGURE 4.1   Swing your arms side-to-side in front of your hips.

UPPER-BODY POSITIONING

It's very important to keep your head up and watch where you're going, not looking down at your skates. Always be aware of where you are going and what obstacles may be ahead of you.

Your shoulders and hips should be square to the direction you are moving. A slight forward lean is necessary, but avoid slouching forward at the hips or shoulders.

LOWER-BODY POSITIONING

The most important part of proper posture is the positioning of your legs and skates. Your legs should be bent at the knee and bent forward at the ankle so you can feel your ankle pressing against the tongue of your boot. With your ankles and knees bent forward, your weight will be over the balls of your feet.

Think of your legs as shock absorbers. As you're skating, you will encounter changes in speed and terrain, inclines and declines, bumps and curbs. Your knees and ankles are the joints that allow your legs to flex and absorb the change in conditions.

STANCE

Stance, or the positioning of your skates on the ground, is measured in width and length. Width refers to the side-to-side distance between your skates, and length describes the forward and backward separation of your skates.

WIDTH OF STANCE

Your skates should be positioned directly under your hips approximately 8 to 12 inches apart (see figure 4.2). The width of your stance will vary if you are stroking. It is common to see new in-line skaters skating with a very wide stance, which undermines the ability to make fluid and stable strokes, turns, and stops.

FIGURE 4.2 A good solid stance will put your skates about 8 to 12 inches apart.

LENGTH OF STANCE

Maintaining proper length of stance is one of the most important fundamentals of in-line skating. Length of stance simply refers to the distance between one skate, which is slightly ahead of your body, and the other skate, which is slightly behind. The proper stance for skating is called the *extended length stance*.

Adding length to your stance has a dramatic stabilizing effect on your skating (see figure 4.3). While standing or coasting, you're much more stable when one foot is ahead of the other than when they are side-by-side. A staggered skate stance makes it much more difficult to fall forward or backward, and your legs can absorb shock more easily in this stance.

71

FIGURE 4.3   A longer stance is more stable than a side-by-side stance.

Imagine a bicycle with two wheels side-by-side, instead of one in front of the other. Trying to stay balanced on the side-by-side bike would be like riding a unicycle: The slightest off-center movement would throw you either forward or backward. However, as soon as you move one of the wheels even slightly ahead of the other, your stability is dramatically increased. The same is true on in-line skates—increasing the length of your wheel base increases your stability.

The length of your stance can vary depending on the skating conditions. When you are standing still, one skate may be 3 to 4 inches in front of the other. When coasting, the heel of the front skate will be approximately even with toe of the back skate. When executing a high-speed turn, there might be as much as two skate lengths between skates.

WEIGHT DISTRIBUTION AND RELAXATION

Your weight should stay evenly distributed between skates, even though they are separated. As your skill level increases, you will learn to shift your weight from one skate to another as you execute different maneuvers such as strokes, turns, and stops. These techniques will be discussed in upcoming chapters.

It's also important to stay relaxed while skating. As you learn about posture and positioning, you must keep in mind that these positions are not absolutely fixed. Your body is constantly changing relative to the terrain, your speed, and the maneuver you are executing. If you are skating with a stiff body, you'll be unable to absorb shocks and adjust to the changing conditions. This stiffness is a result of trying too hard to control your skates, and it will result in fatigued muscles much sooner than skating that is more relaxed and fluid.

In-line skating, like skiing, is a sport more of technique than of strength. Don't force it. Practice and relax.

© K2/Kenneth Redding

Drills

KEEPING YOUR WEIGHT FORWARD

Location: Non-rolling surface (grass or carpet).

1. Look forward and focus on an object 15 to 20 feet in front of you.
2. Square your shoulders to the direction you are facing.
3. Keep arms and hands out in front of your body.
4. Keep hips directly over your skates with upper body slightly forward.
5. Knees should be relaxed and slightly bent.
6. Bend ankles forward. Feel the tongue of the boot against your ankle.
7. Skates should be no more than 12 inches apart (width of stance).

© David Robbins

LEGS AS SHOCK ABSORBERS

Location: Non-rolling surface (grass or carpet).

1. Maintain the same position over skates as described in "Keeping Your Weight Forward."
2. Bend ankles forward.
3. Bend knees.
4. Lower hips, but do not bend forward at the hip. Bend knees until thighs are almost parallel with the floor, but no farther.
5. Move up and down several times.

© David Robbins

SIDE-TO-SIDE ARM SWING

Location: Non-rolling surface (grass or carpet).

1. Maintain the position described in Keeping Your Weight Forward.
2. Slowly swing both arms in unison, left-to-right then right-to-left.
3. Do not allow your hands or arms to swing behind your hips.

EXTENDED LENGTH STANCE

Location: Non-rolling surface (grass or carpet).

1. Maintain same position as described in Keeping Your Weight Forward (width of stance no more than 12 inches).
2. Slide right skate forward one skate length; right knee will straighten slightly (see figure 4.3 on page 72).
3. Slide left skate back one skate length; left knee will bend slightly.
4. Slide the right skate back and left skate forward at the same time (alternate positions).
5. Practice alternating forward skates several times.

Common Mistakes and How to Correct Them

1. Skates feel like they are going to zoom out in front of you:

Your weight is too far back, your hands are swinging behind your hips and/or knees, or your ankles are not bent forward. Swing hands and arms side-to-side, and do not allow your hands to swing behind your hips. Feel your ankles press against the tongue of the boot. Move your skates into a stance with extended length for more stability.

2. Trouble maintaining side-to-side balance while alternating forward skate:

Width of stance may be too close; skates should pass each other 8 to 12 inches apart. Standing with rigid knees and ankles can also contribute to balance problems. Keep knees and ankles bent forward while allowing them to flex with changes in position.

CHAPTER 5

SKATING CORRECTLY

© K2/Kenneth Redding

Skating correctly on in-line skates requires an understanding of the stroke and glide style of skating versus the stroke and stroke style that many beginners use. In-line skating requires the creation of movement, generally by either the skater's legs pushing the skater forward or gravity pulling the skater. When the skater's legs are pushing, only one leg can push at a time: The other leg must support the skater's body and glide along the skating surface.

Skill Checklist

To be sure you have a practical understanding of the stroke and glide style, read this chapter carefully and practice the drills at the end of the chapter until you feel comfortable doing them. Practice skating in a level, open location where you can practice the following skills.

1. Stroke with one leg and balance and glide on the other skate.

2. Execute a consecutive stroke and glide, alternating legs.

3. Stroke and glide, then coast with extended length stance.

4. Alternate forward skate when coasting.

THE STROKE

The stroke is a skater's source of movement, so it is important that you establish a solid foundation by learning it correctly from the outset.

CREATING FORWARD MOTION

Stroke and glide simply means that one skate is stroking outward and slightly back, pushing you forward while the other skate is gliding, or coasting, and taking advantage of that forward momentum. An ideal stroke and glide combination is one that creates the maximum amount of forward momentum while using the least amount of physical energy. We refer to this as an efficient stroke.

In addition to being efficient, a full stroke and recovery of the skate to the original position will provide the maximum amount of muscle use for those skaters who are working on toning and shaping the muscle groups in the upper legs and buttocks.

You may not be very concerned about forward movement at this stage of learning, but remember: This is the foundation of your skating, and the techniques you learn now will stay with you as long as you skate.

BODY POSITION

In chapter 4, you learned the importance of staying balanced and centered over your skates. The same lessons hold true while stroking, with the refinement of shifting and centering your body weight over the glide skate.

If you imagine a vertical line dividing your body in half, it should be perfectly aligned with the center of your glide skate (see figure 5.1). Achieving this alignment will require moving your body over and above the glide skate.

Stay relaxed and bend your knees and ankles forward. Your shoulders and hips should remain square to the direction you are facing; keep your head up and look forward.

STROKE TECHNIQUE

The outward stroke is an extension of your leg that pushes your body forward, creating movement (see figure 5.1). The stroke extends out and away from your body at approximately a 45-degree angle behind you.

81

© K2/Kenneth Redding

FIGURE 5.1 The vertical line shows proper body position—the upper body and knee are aligned above the glide skate's wheels. The stroke will extend at a 45-degree angle behind your body.

As you begin to take a stroke, your body weight shifts to the nonstroke (glide) skate. Your stroke creates movement, causing you to coast on the glide skate. As you glide, you bring the stroke skate back in and underneath your body. Then you shift your weight to the stroke skate, which now becomes the glide skate, and you stroke with the previous glide skate.

WIDTH OF STANCE WHILE STROKING

The width of your stance will remain 8 to 12 inches as described in chapter 4. If you widen your stance beyond that, you will not be able to fully extend your stroke skate, because you will not be able to shift all of your weight to the glide skate.

CHAPTER 6

STOPPING

© David Robbins

The most common question asked by new in-line skaters is, "How do I stop?" It is easy to see similarities between in-line skating and other sports such as roller skating, ice skating, and skiing. However, stopping is an exception to those similarities. This is not to say that stopping is hard—it's just different, and requires that you practice to gain confidence and proficiency.

Skill Checklist

To be sure you have an understanding of different stopping styles, read this chapter carefully and then practice the drills at the end of the chapter until you feel comfortable doing them. Be sure to wear all your safety gear and practice in a level, open location.

1. When using the brake stop, keep your hands up and in front of you and lower your rear end.

2. For T-stops, keep your body weight over the glide skate and drag the other skate at a 90-degree angle behind you.

3. For Y-stops, keep your body weight over the glide skate and drag the other skate at a 45-degree angle behind you.

4. For advanced hockey stops, execute a sharp turn to the right or left (see chapter 7 for instruction on executing turns).

BRAKE STOP

On most in-line skates, the brake is located behind the back wheel on the right skate. Some in-line skates have brakes on both skates, and some more advanced skates do not have a brake at all. On skates with the brake on only one side, the brake can be moved to either skate, allowing you to use your stronger leg.

If you've roller skated and are accustomed to rolling up onto a toe stop, you'll want to relearn quickly. Rolling up on your toes on in-line skates will send you tumbling on your chin!

We will assume that, as with most in-line skates, your brake is on the back of your right skate.

BODY POSITION

The proper stopping position on in-line skates can be described as an outgrowth of the extended length stance. In the extended length stance with the right skate forward, applying the brake requires lifting the right toe until the brake pad contacts the ground and creates enough friction to slow you down (see figure 6.1).

FIGURE 6.1 With the brake skate forward, lift your toe to apply the brake.

If you're coasting in the extended length stance, shift the majority of your weight to your left skate and drop your rear end slightly toward the ground. This dropping is the same movement as sitting down in a chair; it provides more leverage against the brake and allows you to stop faster. The drop will require bending the left knee. As you lift the right skate's toe to apply the brake, your right knee will straighten (see figure 6.2). Your arms and hands should be up and out in front of your body. This position will help offset the forward momentum of your upper body as your skates slow down.

As you practice the brake stop and gain confidence, you will be able to stop from increasingly higher speeds. As your speed goes up, you will have to lower your body more in order to apply greater pressure to the brake.

© David Robbins

FIGURE 6.2 Lower your body before you apply the brake while coasting.

STOPPING ON HILLS

The key to stopping on hills is maintaining control of speed. New in-line skaters are often surprised at how fast in-line skates can accelerate down hills. Anticipate your potential acceleration and start applying your brakes early to keep the speed down. Your brakes could also be applied continuously to help control speed. If you gain too much speed and begin to lose control, try to turn and traverse the side of the hill (see chapter 8).

As you approach any hill it is critically important to assess your prior experience and skills before descending. Do not attempt to skate down a hill if you don't feel confident controlling your speed. Take off your skates and walk down if you need to, or slip a device over your wheels that enables you to walk up and down hills (see figure 6.3).

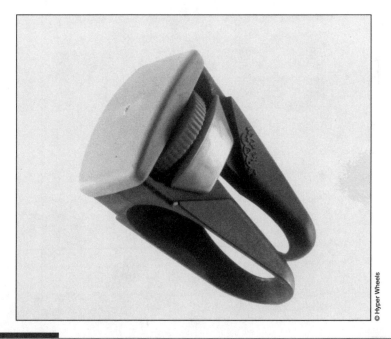

© Hyper Wheels

FIGURE 6.3   Slip this device over your wheels so you can walk up and down hills.

T-STOP

The brake stop is the most common stop. However, there are some conditions that will require an alternate technique. The most common alternative is the T-stop (see figure 6.4), which gets its name from the position of the skates.

The T-stop is executed by dragging one skate behind the other at a 90-degree angle to the direction you're going. Applying pressure to the inside edges of the wheels on the skate that is being dragged will slow you down.

When skating, you will encounter situations that force you to stop quickly, perhaps to avoid another person or obstacle. Knowing how to execute two different types of stops will help you stop more quickly. In the brake stop, your skate must

© David Robbins

FIGURE 6.4 The drag skate is at a 90-degree angle to the direction of movement when you execute a T-stop.

move out in front of you to execute the stop, but in the T-stop, the skate moves behind you. These differences allow you more versatility depending on the position of your body and legs at the time you realize you must stop. It does take time and practice for these two styles of stopping to become instinctive, but keep practicing both and you'll acquire that instinct.

The one disadvantage to using the T-stop is wearing out wheels. You are using the inside edges of the wheels as stoppers, and it's easy to rub a flat spot into the wheels. You can reduce the amount of wear by allowing yourself more space to slow down and not applying as much hard pressure.

Most skaters favor dragging one skate over the other. If you feel more comfortable balancing on your right skate and dragging your left, practice the T-stop that way. Practice the T-stop with increasing speed each time until you feel comfortable and confident executing the stop.

ADVANCED STOPS

There are other ways of stopping on in-line skates. These stops are more advanced and should only be tried by skaters with a high degree of skill.

Y-STOP

When executing a Y-stop, set one skate slightly behind you at a 45-degree angle (see figure 6.5a through d). This positioning of the skate will cause you to turn sharply. The friction of a sharp turn will slow you down.

HOCKEY STOP

Hockey stops on in-line skates are more difficult than on ice skates. A hockey stop, on ice, is a quick, sharp turn that causes the skate blades to slide sideways across the ice. On in-line skates, the wheels are sticky and the skating surface is rougher than ice. The combination of wheels and surface creates more traction and makes it difficult for the wheels to break away and slide sideways across cement or asphalt.

a. Bend your left knee and ankle forward.

b. Shift body weight to the left skate.

FIGURE 6.5   The Y-stop is like the T-stop except for the angle of the stroke skate.

c. Move your right skate behind left skate at a 45-degree angle pressing down on the right skate.

© David Robbins

d. Allow your left skate to turn to the right so your body pivots around the right skate and you rotate to a stop.

© David Robbins

FIGURE 6.5 *continued*

Hockey stops can be executed on in-line skates, but it takes a high level of skill and speed to get the skates to break away and slide. Because of this, we advise against using the hockey stop unless you are a very advanced skater.

Before attempting a hockey stop, you should be comfortable with turning in the extended length stance (chapter 7). To execute the stop, simply make a sharp, fast turn in either direction. As you make the turn, lean your body in and push your skates away from the center of the turn, forcing the wheels to slide across the surface.

There is a fine line between a controlled slide and a fall, so be sure to have all safety gear on and be comfortable and confident with your turns before attempting this stop. This is the least common way to stop on in-line skates and should only be attempted by advanced skaters.

SKATE AND BODY POSITION WHILE USING BRAKE

Location: Non-rolling surface (grass or carpet).

1. Look forward and focus on an object 15 to 20 feet in front of you.

2. Square your shoulders to the direction you are facing.

3. Put your hands and arms up and in front of you, chest high.

4. Move skates into extended length stance with the right skate forward.

5. Shift your body weight to the left skate and lower your rear end.

6. Lift the toe of your right skate until you feel pressure on the brake.

7. Maintain balance in this position.

8. Practice moving from a gliding position to the brake position several times.

STOPPING WITH THE BRAKE

Location: Flat, open, hard rolling surface.

1. Put on all safety gear as described in chapter 2.
2. Execute three consecutive stroke and glide combinations.
3. Move into the extended length stance with the right skate forward.
4. Shift your body weight to the left skate and lower your rear end.
5. Lift the toe of your right skate and apply pressure on the brake (see figures 6.1 and 6.2 on pages 89 and 90).
6. Stop.
7. Practice several times, gradually increasing speed.

SKATE AND BODY POSITION FOR T-STOP AND Y-STOP

Location: Non-rolling surface (grass or carpet).

1. Look forward and focus on an object 15 to 20 feet in front of you.
2. Square your shoulders to the direction you're facing.
3. Put your hands and arms up and in front of you.
4. Bend your left knee and ankle forward.
5. Shift your body weight to the left skate.
6. Move the right skate behind the left skate at a 90-degree angle (45-degree angle for Y-Stop).
7. Apply downward pressure to the wheels on the right skate.

T-STOP

Location: Flat, open, hard rolling surface.

1. Put on all safety gear as described in chapter 2.
2. Execute three consecutive stroke and glide combinations.
3. Bend your left knee and ankle forward.
4. Shift your body weight to the left skate.
5. Move the right skate behind the left skate at a 90-degree angle.
6. Apply downward pressure to the wheels on your right skate.
7. Stop.
8. Practice several times, gradually increasing speed.

Y-STOP

Location: Flat, open, hard rolling surface.

1. Put on all safety gear as described in chapter 2.
2. Execute three consecutive stroke and glide combinations.
3. Bend your left knee and ankle forward.
4. Shift your body weight to the left skate.
5. Move the right skate behind the left skate at a 45-degree angle (see figure 6.5 on pages 94 and 95).
6. Apply downward pressure to the wheels on your right skate.
7. Allow your left skate to turn to the right so that your body pivots around the right skate.
8. Spin to a stop.

HOCKEY STOP

Location: Flat, open, hard rolling surface.

1. Put on all safety gear as described in chapter 2.
2. Execute three consecutive stroke and glide combinations.
3. Move your right skate slightly forward into an extended length stance.
4. Execute a very sharp right turn, pushing hard against the skates so they slide across the skating surface.
5. Stop.

Common Mistakes and How to Correct Them

1. Feeling of falling backward when stopping with the brake:

Keep your hands and arms up and in front of your body. This will help offset the slight backward lean that your body has when braking.

2. Pivoting or turning around the brake when stopping with the brake:

Your stance is too wide. The braking skate must be directly in front of you when stopping or you'll pivot around the brake (see figure 6.6). Review Width of Stance in chapter 4.

© David Robbins

| FIGURE 6.6 | If your stance is too wide when executing a brake stop, you will rotate around the brake. |

3. Pivoting or spinning when setting down drag skate for a T-stop:

Your drag skate is not at a 90-degree angle to the direction you're moving. Set the skate down directly behind the forward-facing skate at a 90-degree angle.

TURNS

© David Robbins

Executing consistent, smooth turns on in-line skates is one of the most rewarding parts of skating. Most skiers will tell you that carving long, fluid turns through a field of fresh powder snow is the best part of skiing. Many in-line skaters experience the same feeling while carving turns on their skates.

Skill Checklist

To be sure you have a practical understanding of the mechanics of turning and the different types of turns, read this chapter carefully and practice the drills at the end of the chapter until you feel comfortable doing them.

1. Maintain a consistent arc.

2. Increase speed of turns.

3. Connect right and left turns.

4. Execute crossover turns.

5. Traverse down hills.

THE LEADING SKATE

The extended length stance is the key to successful turns. When coasting with one skate in front of the other, the front skate will lead you into the turn. If you want to turn right, your right skate should be forward; to turn left, your left skate should be forward. Always put the inside skate forward (see figure 7.1).

If you are not comfortable coasting in the extended length stance, go back to chapter 4 and practice alternating the forward skate.

FIGURE 7.1 In-line wheels will stick to the ground even when you're leaning into a turn.

You may have already developed a habit of turning with the outside skate forward. This is common among skiers who are in-line skating because they have learned to turn with the outside ski forward. If you do turn in this manner, you'll need to spend time breaking the habit. It will be challenging to learn the proper form, but is worth the effort to ensure more stability and control while skating.

THE MECHANICS OF TURNS

Before you begin practicing turns, it is important to understand the basic techniques that are involved in executing turns:

● Trust your edges. Skiers and ice skaters are familiar with using edges in turns. Skis and ice skates have sharp 90-degree edges on the outside and inside of the bottom of the ski or skate. These sharp edges help hold the skis and skates to the slick surface when carving a turn. The wheels on in-lines skates have no edges, but they do have rounded sides on the wheels that grip the skating surface instead of sliding when turning. The wheel design of in-line skates allows you to lean the skate over without it slipping out from under you.

● Lean into the turn. To turn successfully on in-line skates, you must lean into the turn. It is nearly impossible to make an efficient turn without leaning into it (see figure 7.1 on page 103).

● Look forward. You should always be looking in the direction you want to go. If you are looking down at your skates, you cannot be preparing for the next turn. Look in the direction of your turn. Your body goes where your eyes go.

● Keep your shoulders turned in. Turn your shoulders in the direction you're turning, and slightly drop the inside shoulder. For example, if you're turning to the right, turn your shoulders in to the right and drop your right shoulder slightly. This dropping of the right shoulder will force you to lean into the turn.

● Avoid favoring either direction. It's common for skaters and skiers to favor turning in one direction over the other. Do your best, through practice, to overcome this favoritism as you will need to be confident in turning in either direction.

CONNECTING TURNS

After you have gained confidence in turning both to the left and to the right, you will want to begin connecting turns. Learning how to connect turns is the beginning of truly fun in-line skating. These fundamental skills will be used in all types of advanced skating.

TRANSITION OF THE FORWARD SKATE

The key to connecting turns is changing the forward skate after the preceding turn is completed. If you begin with a right turn, the right skate is forward and you are leaning to the right. As you come out of the turn, your body will straighten to a vertical position. Shift your stance so your left skate is forward and leads you into the left turn.

For additional information on the transition of the forward skate, refer to the chapter 5 drill Coasting: Extended Length Stance on page 85. Practice alternating your forward skate while coasting.

MAINTAINING PROPER POSTURE

Proper posture remains important as your turning skills develop. As you make the transition from one turn to the next, maintain the forward bend in your knees and ankles. Remember that your inside, or forward, knee will have more forward bend and will lead you into and through the turn.

INCREASING SPEED

As you gain confidence in turning, you will approach turns with greater speed. With increased speed, you will have to change three things to maintain the same arc through a turn:

● Extend the length of your stance. Move your forward skate out farther forward and your back skate back a little more. This change in the length of stance will require more bend in the forward knee and the back ankle.

● Lower your body closer to the ground. Extending the length of your stance will lower your body closer to the ground, allowing you to complete faster turns. The lower your center of gravity is, the faster you can turn (see figure 7.2).

● Increase weight and pressure on the inside leg. As you enter a turn at a higher speed, your forward knee will push down, forward, and into the turn. You will feel more weight and pressure applied to the knee on your forward leg. You are forced to drive the forward knee into the turn.

As you practice these turns, remember: Chances are good that you have not reached the limits of your skates and that they will not slide out from under you. There is a limit to how far you can push the skates, but most skaters do not reach that limit until they dramatically increase their speed.

© Hyper Wheels

FIGURE 7.2   The faster the turn, the lower your body should be.

CROSSOVER TURNS

The crossover turn is a combination stroke and turn that is used in roller skating, ice skating, and in-line skating (see figure 7.3a through d on page 108). The benefit of the crossover is that by using it, you can increase your speed while you're turning.

In chapter 5, you learned that you can balance on one skate while the other skate is extended in the stroke position. A crossover requires balancing on one skate while turning and then alternating the skate you're balanced on, shifting your body weight and balance. This may sound intimidating, but you can learn to crossover one step at a time.

THE STEPS OF A CROSSOVER

Crossovers can be broken into three different segments: the stepover, the understroke, and the topstroke. It is important to remember that the crossover is executed during a turn and not while coasting in a straight line.

The Stepover

Remember, in turning, the inside skate is always in front of the body and the outside skate is behind. Be sure to maintain a forward bend in the knee and ankle, as that will make the stepover easier. Shift your weight to the forward skate and pick up the back skate and cross it over in front of and slightly inside of the forward skate (see figure 7.3a through c). In a right turn, for example, the right skate is forward. To begin the stepover, shift your body weight to the right skate and pick up your left skate, swing it over and in front of the right skate, and set it down in front of and slightly inside of your right skate.

The Understroke

You can complete the crossover step simply by stepping over as described above without stroking underneath your body. But the understroke, though not required to complete a crossover, is a powerful and efficient stroke. It takes time and practice to learn the understroke, but most advanced skaters agree that it is one of the most useful methods of increasing speed.

Under normal stroke and glide conditions, your right leg strokes out to the right of your body. In a right crossover turn, however, you need to stroke your right leg underneath you and toward the left side of your body at the same time as the stepover (see figure 7.3c). As you complete the understroke, shift your body weight to the skate that has just completed the stepover.

The Topstroke

After completing the stepover and understroke, your weight has been shifted to your stepover skate (see figure 7.3d). The understroke skate begins to recover back to the original side of the body and the stepover skate begins to push out in a normal stroking direction. This push of the stepover skate is

a. Get into the extended length stance with the right skate forward.

b. Pick up the extended left leg.

| FIGURE 7.3 | The steps of a right crossover turn. |

c. Cross it over the bent right leg (the step-over) while pushing off in the opposite direction (the understroke) with your right leg.

d. Your balance will now switch to your left leg (d) and your right leg will recover to the right side of the body. Your left skate will start normal stroking (the topstroke).

FIGURE 7.3 *continued*

called the topstroke. For example, in a right crossover turn, your weight shifts to your left skate upon completion of the stepover. Your understroke (right) skate begins to recover to the right side of your body and your left skate begins to push out to your left to complete the topstroke. As you execute the topstroke with your left skate, your skates are in position to begin another crossover.

TIPS FOR CROSSOVER PERFORMANCE

Crossover steps can be quick, short steps or fully extended, long strokes; it depends on your turning radius, speed, and desired acceleration. Practice the crossover turn in both directions. In a right turn, the stepover is done with the left skate, the understroke with the right skate, and the topstroke with the left skate. For a left turn, stepover with the right skate, understroke with the left skate, and topstroke with the right skate. It may be easier to learn the crossover turn with a slow, wide turning arc.

Crossovers can be executed at any time during a turn. Remember the fundamentals you have previously learned. Keep your weight forward on the balls of your feet, look in the direction you want to turn, angle your shoulders into the turn, and keep your inside skate forward. Stay relaxed and practice.

TRAVERSING DOWN HILLS

Traversing on hills is a technique adapted from skiing that allows in-line skaters to maintain control of their speed while skating down hills. Traversing is a series of connecting right and left turns that allows you to skate across a hill instead of straight down it.

To understand traversing, imagine yourself standing at the top of a wide cement hill. If you were to drop a ball and let

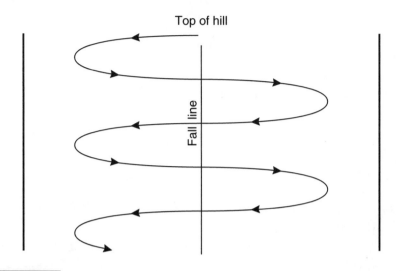

Top of hill

Fall line

FIGURE 7.4 The straight line down the hill (the fall line) is the fastest way to the bottom. The crisscross (traversing) line is the best route for controlling speed down hills.

it roll to the bottom of the hill, gravity would pull it the fastest route down the hill. This is called the fall line. If you were to coast down the hill on your skates, you would follow the same line. Traversing allows you to slow your descent. The key is to crisscross back and forth across the fall line (see figure 7.4).

To traverse, skate across the side of a hill, then make a U-turn and go back across the hill in the opposite direction. After crossing the hill, execute another U-turn and head back in the original direction. Continue the zigzag pattern to the bottom of the hill.

If you begin to gain too much speed while traversing, you can make a complete turn plus a little more and actually skate back up the hill slightly. This will reduce your speed.

Drills

Remember to put on all safety gear as described in Chapter 2.

RIGHT AND LEFT TURNS

Location: Flat, open, hard rolling surface with markers set up as shown.

1. Execute three consecutive stroke and glide combinations.
2. Move into the extended length stance with the right skate forward.
3. Begin to lean into the turn.
4. Slightly lower your right shoulder.
5. Keep your eyes on the center marker.
6. Maintain a smooth turn around the arc of the cones.
7. Practice a left turn following steps 1 through 6, with the left skate leading into the turn.

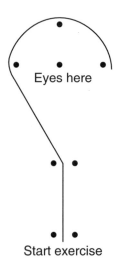

Eyes here

Start exercise

CONNECTING RIGHT AND LEFT TURNS

Location: Flat, open, hard rolling surface with markers set up as shown.

1. Execute stroke and glide combinations to build speed.
2. Move into the extended length stance with your right skate forward.
3. Execute a turn.
4. Shift the left skate to the forward position and the right skate back.
5. Execute another turn.
6. Shift the right skate to the forward position and the left skate back.
7. Execute another turn.

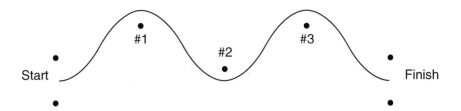

Variation:

After completing the Connecting Right and Left Turns drill, you can improve your skill by increasing your speed through the same course. Remember to lengthen your stance and lower your body closer to the ground. Drive into the turn with the inside, forward knee.

CROSSOVER TURNS

Location: Flat, open, hard rolling surface.

1. Execute three consecutive stroke and glide combinations.
2. Move into the extended length stance with your right skate forward. (See figure 7.3a on page 108).
3. Begin a coasting turn to the right.
4. Shift your weight to the right skate.
5. Lift the left skate, cross it over and in front of the right skate, and set it down (figure 7.3b and c).
6. Shift your weight to the left skate.
7. Push under your body and toward the left with your right skate (figure 7.3d).
8. Begin to return the right skate to normal position.
9. Begin a left skate stroke to the left.
10. Set the right skate down and shift your weight to it.
11. Complete the extension of your left skate and lift it. Move your left skate directly into the stepover.
12. Complete the entire crossover maneuver a second time.

Common Mistakes and How to Correct Them

1. Not able to maintain arc of turn around markers:

Keep your inside skate forward. Lean into the turn.

2. Ankles feel unstable when trying to turn:

Your skates might not be tight enough around your ankles or might be too big. Tighten your laces or buckles and check for correct size.

CHAPTER 8

PUTTING IT ALL TOGETHER

© K2/Scott Markewitz

In-line skating is a process of constant adaptation to changing conditions. Speed, terrain, and body position can change at any moment. You have learned the individual basic skills that will enable you to respond to these changes. But before you can quickly and confidently adjust to changing conditions, all of the fundamentals must become instinctive. The key to developing this skill is practice!

Skill Checklist

To be sure you have an understanding of how all the skills we have covered so far come together, read this chapter carefully and practice the drills at the end of the chapter until you feel comfortable doing them.

1. Connect all basic skills—stroke, glide, coasting turns, crossover turns, and stops.

2. Skating up hills: Keep weight slightly back and glide up the hill on the forward momentum of your skates.

3. Skating down hills: Analyze the situation to determine the appropriate speed-controlling technique.

4. Skating up curbs: Step up one skate at a time as if you were running.

5. Skating down curbs: Use an extended length stance to skate off and land.

6. Skating backward: Keep your knees bent and weight on the balls of your feet; relax.

7. Toe-heel glide: Maintain an extended length stance and keep your knees bent.

8. Toe-toe glide: Maintain an extended length stance and keep your knees bent.

Nothing will accelerate your learning curve faster than spending time on your skates. Find time in your busy life to skate, relax, and enjoy your newfound sport. If you respond like most people, you'll get hooked, and skating will become a recreational priority.

To maximize the effectiveness of your practice, create a practice course that demands all of your new skills. A drill for practicing appears on page 124.

CHANGING CONDITIONS

Under some conditions, the basic techniques taught in previous chapters will require minor changes. The following sections describe some of these changes.

SKATING UP HILLS

When skating up hills, you should shift your weight back on your skates slightly. This is a minor change from the normal skating posture of keeping your weight over the balls of your feet, but it does not represent a major change in balance. This weight shift will allow you to coast up the hill with less resistance, allowing you to create the maximum amount of forward momentum with the least amount of energy. If you are skating up a steep hill, use a shorter than normal stroke and try to maximize the glide time.

SKATING DOWN HILLS

Skating down hills can be intimidating. Staying in control when skating down a hill requires an analysis of both the hill and your skating skills. The questions you must consider include: Is the paved surface on this hill wide enough to traverse? Is the hill too steep for me to negotiate at my current skill level? If you are faced with a hill that is above your skill or confidence level, take your skates off and walk to the bottom. Better safe than sorry.

SKATING UP CURBS

Going up a curb on in-line skates is no different than going up a curb while walking or running. As you approach the curb with both skates on the ground, shift your weight to one skate and lift the other skate and step up on the curb (see figure 8.1). When the step-up skate is set down, shift your weight to it and lift the back skate up to follow.

It's best to practice these step-ups slowly at first. As you gain more confidence and approach curbs at a faster speed, you will need to lift the first skate up sooner, and the back skate may leave the ground before you set the front skate down. So the transition is really a small hop in the air. It may sound frightening, but if you compare skating up a curb with

| FIGURE 8.1 | Shift your weight to one skate and lift the other up and over the curb. |

running up one, you'll realize it's not as hard as it sounds. When running, you often make the transition of weight from back foot to front foot when both feet are off the ground. This transition on in-line skates is almost identical. Practice slowly and build your confidence.

SKATING OFF CURBS

When approaching a curb that you must go down, you have two choices: You can either stop and step down the curb, or you can maintain your forward speed and skate off the curb. If you decide to skate off the curb, approach it in the extended length stance with both skates on the ground for maximum stability (see figure 8.2). Maintain a speed at which you feel comfortable and in control.

© David Robbins

FIGURE 8.2   When skating off curbs, maintain an extended length stance for added stability when landing.

119

As you go off the curb, do not add a jump: Just skate straight off while maintaining the same posture. When you land, allow your knees and ankles to bend forward to absorb the shock. Land with your skates in an extended length stance, again for additional stability.

BASIC TRICKS

The following sections will introduce you to a few basic tricks and advanced skating. Many of these skills will be used in other styles of advanced skating as discussed in Part III. As with all skills, the key is practice!

SKATING BACKWARD

Skating backward is one of the first things most skaters want to learn once they have mastered the fundamental skills. Skating backward can be intimidating, but it is not difficult to do. The basic rules of keeping your knees and ankles bent forward and your weight over the balls of your feet do not change when skating backward (see figure 8.3).

Start with your back facing in the direction you want to go. Stand with the toes of your skates facing slightly inward, and keep your knees and ankles bent forward. To create movement, push both skates out at the same time to about 3 feet apart, then turn your heels inward and bring the skates back together. Repeating this movement will create hourglass figures with your skates and propel you backward. Keeping your hands and arms out in front of you will help you maintain balance.

As you become more proficient at skating backward, you can increase speed with the same type of stroke with some slight modifications. As you skate backward, move your skates into an extended length stance and begin the hourglass stroke. As your skates come to the center, allow them to cross, one behind the other. You will now be creating a figure-eight pattern instead of an hourglass. This additional range of movement will allow you to put more power into the stroke and to create more speed.

© Lesley Ellam

FIGURE 8.3 Notice how this skater looks like he's ready to sit down. Excellent form (note his skate spread) for skating backwards!

Changing from a backward skating position to a forward position while moving requires a step-around. Begin by shifting your weight to your right skate, then lift your left skate and begin turning the toe out to the left. As your toe and leg turn out, your hips, torso, shoulders, and head will also begin to turn. When your left skate is pointing in the opposite direction of your right skate, set the left skate down and begin to shift your weight to the left skate. As your weight shifts, lift your right skate and bring it around and parallel to the left skate. This all happens as one fluid motion that is initiated by the turning out of your left toe.

At first, skating backward does not feel natural and many skaters are uncomfortable with it. Stay loose and relaxed, keep practicing, and you'll pick it up quickly.

121

TOE-HEEL GLIDE

The toe-heel glide is another relatively easy maneuver that looks quite impressive. This trick is done by gliding on the back (heel) wheel of your forward skate and the front (toe) wheel of your back skate. The key to staying balanced is maintaining an extended length stance and keeping your knees bent (see figure 8.4).

TOE-TOE GLIDE

The toe-toe glide is slightly more difficult than the toe-heel glide but is also more impressive. The toe-toe glide requires and builds strength in the calf muscles. As with other maneuvers, the key to staying balanced is maintaining an extended length stance and keeping your knees bent (see figure 8.5).

EXPANDING YOUR SKILLS

Now that you have a solid foundation of in-line skating skills, you are faced with some decisions about your skating future. Many skaters are satisfied with the recreational skating skills they have developed. Those skaters will still have all of the benefits of exercise and a fun new sport. However, many skaters want more out of the sport.

Part III will introduce you to the most popular advanced forms of in-line skating: racing, aggressive skating, and roller hockey. The following chapters will provide instruction on the fundamental skills needed to participate in these variations of in-line skating.

If you decide to seriously pursue any advanced aspect of in-line skating, you need to get actively involved with other enthusiasts. Check your local skate shop and find out if they can put you in touch with skaters who have similar interests, or refer to appendix B of this book (page 186) to find out how to contact organizations that focus on your area of interest.

If you cannot find the resources you want, take the initiative and form a practice group or club in your area to serve your special interests. The national groups listed in appendix B will often help in the organization of a local club or group.

FIGURE 8.4   A toe-heel glide demonstrates the e-x-t-e-n-d-e-d l-e-n-g-t-h stance.

FIGURE 8.5   Gliding toe to toe also requires an extended length stance—just not as much.

As your skills increase and your horizons expand, remember that you have developed a solid foundation of skills. Whatever direction you decide to go with your skating, those fundamentals will not change.

Drills

Remember to put on all safety gear as described in Chapter 2.

KEEPING YOUR WEIGHT FORWARD

Objective: Putting fundamental skills together.

Location: Flat, open, hard rolling surface with markers set up as shown.

1. Start stroke and glide.
2. Connect five alternating coasting turns.
3. Stop, using the brake.
4. Stroke and glide.
5. Connect three alternating crossover turns.
6. Stop, using a T– or Y–stop.
7. Skate to finish.

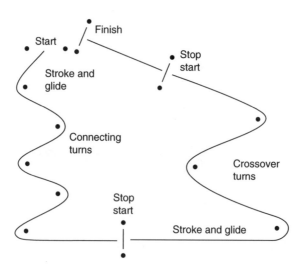

Variation:

Try timing yourself and friends with a stopwatch. As you practice, your reactions to changes in the course will start to become instinctive.

SKATING UP CURBS

Location: Flat, open, hard rolling surface with a curb leading to a sidewalk.

1. Start stroke and glide.
2. Approach the curb with both skates on the ground.
3. Shift weight to one skate.
4. Step above curb level with the other skate and set it down. (See figure 8.1 on page 118).
5. Shift weight to the upper skate.
6. Lift the back skate up to follow.

SKATING OFF CURBS

Location: Flat, open, sidewalk with curb leading to a lower surface.

1. Start stroke and glide to a comfortable speed.
2. Approach the curb with both skates on the ground in an extended length stance. (See figure 8.2 on page 119).
3. Skate off the curb, maintaining the extended length stance.
4. Upon landing, allow your knees and ankles to bend forward to absorb the shock.

SKATING BACKWARD

Location: Flat, open, hard rolling surface.

1. Stand with your back facing the direction you want to go.
2. Point toes slightly inward. (See figure 8.3 on page 121)
3. Push both skates out to about 3 feet apart.
4. Bring skates back together.
5. Repeat maneuvers as space allows.
6. As speed increases, coast while skates are parallel.

TOE-HEEL GLIDE

Location: Flat, open, hard rolling surface.

1. Stroke and glide to a comfortable coasting speed.
2. Begin to glide in an extended length stance with at least 18 inches between the front and back skate.
3. Lift the toe of the front skate so you are riding on only the back wheel.
4. Lift the heel of the back skate, keeping your knee bent, and ride on the front wheel.
5. Coast in the heel-toe position. (See figure 8.4 on page 123).

Hint:

If you are putting your right skate out in front, you may rub the brake. Try the maneuver with the left skate in front or remove your brake. Before removing your brake, be sure you can properly execute a T-stop.

TOE-TOE GLIDE

Location: Flat, open, hard rolling surface.

1. Stroke and glide to a comfortable coasting speed.
2. Begin to glide in the extended length stance with at least 12 inches between the front and back skate.
3. Lift the heel of the back skate so you're coasting only on the front (toe) wheel.
4. Lift the heel of the front skate so you're coasting only on the front (toe) wheel.
5. Maintain an extended length stance and keep your knees bent. (See figure 8.5 on page 123).
6. As your speed slows, drop back to flat skates.

Common Mistakes and How to Correct Them

1. Trouble connecting basic skills:

Be sure that you can confidently perform all individual skills before attempting to connect them.

2. Unable to skate up a hill:

Keep your weight slightly back on your heels to avoid pushing the front wheels into the hill.

3. Lacking confidence skating down hills:

Learn on small hills first and gradually work your way up to larger hills. Extremely steep hills may be too dangerous to skate safely.

PART III

ADVANCED IN-LINE SKATING

In-line skating is a diverse sport that millions of people around the world enjoy. The recreational and health benefits of this new sport are phenomenal. Many skaters, after learning the fundamental skills, will want to expand on those skills and explore the more advanced types of skating.

The sport can be divided into four primary disciplines: recreational, racing, aggressive, and hockey. The last three take more advanced skills than recreational skating. In this section, you will be introduced to these three advanced disciplines and will learn the fundamentals of each.

CHAPTER 9

IN-LINE
RACING

Visualize yourself skating a marathon. You're in the middle of a tight pack of about 30 skaters racing along at 25 miles per hour on an open country road, the wind whistling by as you're tucked tight in line—inches from your competitors, sucking up their draft.

The pack is in perfect unison stride for stride, appearing almost as if it were one. The combination of oxygen debt, heat, and the rhythm of the pack causes you to drift into a hypnotic trance. Time passes and the miles go by when suddenly the skater in front of you steps aside, and you snap out of your trance. The pressure's on. It's your turn to take over the lead pulling the pack.

Expecting a strong head wind, you automatically push harder to maintain or increase the pace. But to your surprise, the head wind is gone, replaced by a tail wind as you approach 30 miles per hour with minimal effort. The road slopes into a fairly good downhill grade as you approach speeds in excess of 40 miles per hour—too fast to keep striding efficiently. You settle into a deep downhill-style tuck with your hands together in front of your face, cutting the wind like a knife, in pursuit of the ultimate aerodynamic position. You feel a slight nudge from behind, and suddenly realize that the awesome draft you have created has given the pack an open tunnel with almost no resistance. They have no choice but to either blow by or push you even faster down the hill. You feel like the front bumper on an overloaded semi roaring down a hill with no brakes. The adrenaline rush is overwhelming as you hear one of your competitors howl with mutual excitement.

Looking ahead, you see a large hairpin turn. Based on your preliminary course review, you feel fairly confident that the turn is possible at your current speed. You hit the corner perfectly, but about halfway through, the G-forces cause you to swing wide and hit a fine layer of sand. Starting to lose control, you slide sideways. You tense up, crouch lower, and spread your legs slightly. Suddenly, the wheels grip and give you a jolt, and you're through it with no noticeable loss in speed.

Now the sun is at your back. Still descending, you notice that the shadows from your competitors that should be coming from behind aren't there. Thighs burning from the prolonged low tuck, you get even lower, knowing that if the pack is still together, their speed will rocket them right by, and you'll probably be left in the dust.

Suddenly a shadow appears to your left. Three skaters pass you about 10 feet away. You make a break for it, trying to catch their draft. The seconds tick by, and you don't seem to move at all. Finally the gap starts to narrow. Then you're caught in the vacuum, sucked in at a speed that forces you to decide to either blow by or stand up slightly to catch more air and gradually settle into the back of the pack. You remember the last race, when you made your break too early, and you decide that the pack is the best choice. Now tight in line, relaxed in the draft, you glance back to check out the rest of the pack that was with you going into the hairpin corner. To your surprise the others are several hundred yards behind, and they're split up into small groups.

This is it. It's you and three others and about a mile and a half left with one climb and then a slight downhill finish. You're entering the dip at the base of a hill where it begins to rise. One by one, each skater starts striding until all are in unison. The leader steps aside and there is a sudden increase in speed that requires everything you have just to hang on. With a quick look back, you realize it's one down and two to go.

Still maintaining the brutal near-sprint pace, you feel your legs starting to go. As you approach the top of the hill, the pace slows slightly and you can see the short, choppy, wide strokes with an occasional wobble that signal fatigue in your opponents. The leader who almost broke you pulls aside and doesn't look like he is going to be much of a threat. Now it's you and the new leader, who is picking up the pace at an alarming rate. You tuck your head down and hang, knowing the finish can't be more than 800 yards off. Again approaching 40 miles per hour on a slight decline, you can see the finish line about 100 yards off and decide it's now or never. You back off just slightly—enough to give three power strokes in the draft—slingshot out into the lead and feel the finish ribbon hit your burning thigh.

TYPES OF RACING

Most outdoor and indoor races have beginner and advanced divisions, so don't let the idea of competition dissuade you from trying an in-line race. Whether your intention is to win or just to enjoy the day of organized skating, a common goal shared by all skaters is to have fun!

As the sport of in-line skating grows, so does the interest in racing and speed skating competitions. Over the last few years, people ranging from 5 to 75 years old have tested their endurance and skills against the clock and each other by competing in races from 100 meters to over 100 miles. Almost every major city in the United States holds at least one in-line skating race per year, and that number will increase as the sport grows. For more information on race schedules, contact IISA or USAC/RS (see appendix B, page 186).

If you have a desire to get involved with in-line racing, this chapter will give you an introduction to the competitive aspects of the sport and how to train for them.

SPRINTS

Sprint racing consists of power and leg speed bursting from a standing start. Distances are usually 300 to 1,500 meters. Courses can be on special banked tracks, indoor rinks, or flat surfaces for straight point-to-point drag races. Sprints usually start with groups of 5 to 10 with the best times qualifying for a final round. Competitors are generally racing against the clock as well as each other.

10K

The 10K (10 kilometers) is by far the most popular distance for in-line racing. This is a 6.2-mile race that is usually conducted on a closed-circuit course similar to that for criterium-style bike racing, which is usually two blocks by two blocks if in a city, or around a track if elsewhere (see figure 9.1). Competitors form pace lines to cut down wind resistance and conserve energy. This style of racing is exciting for both participants and spectators, combining strength, speed, endurance, and strategic competitiveness.

FIGURE 9.1   Most 10ks are on a criterium style race course.

© Annelise Cunis

There have been 10K races worldwide with more than 1,000 competitors in a single race, and the majority of them finish in less than 45 minutes. The fastest skaters complete the race in less than 15 minutes. That's averaging over 24.8 miles per hour! Sprints at the end of the race can exceed 30 miles per hour on flat ground.

MARATHON AND OTHER LONG DISTANCE RACES

Marathon racing generally refers to all long distance races that are marathon distance (26.2 miles) and greater. Marathons are growing in popularity as the speeds for 10Ks continue to increase so that they are like a prolonged sprint. Longer-distance races provide the endurance athlete an opportunity to excel.

Marathons range in distance from the traditional 26.2 miles to over 100 miles, depending on the particular race. The most well-known marathon in the United States is the annual 85-mile Athens to Atlanta Ultra Marathon held each October in Georgia. In-line skaters have completed this race in less than 4 1/2 hours!

INDOOR RACING

Indoor racing is a part of the sport that is just opening up for in-line skaters. The United States Amateur Confederation of Roller Skating (USAC/RS) has recently legalized in-line skates for indoor competition. This provides a tremendous opportunity for in-line racers who live in regions with weather patterns that restrict outdoor racing and training during the winter months.

Indoor racing is very different from outdoor racing. The indoor track is usually a 100-meter oval, and the races often feature no more than nine skaters at any time. Races are 300 to 2,000 meters in length, with the most popular being 500 meters. National pace indoor speed skaters on traditional quad skates can skate the five-lap, 500-meter race in under 55 seconds.

The introduction of in-line skates into indoor rink racing is having a major impact on this well-established sport. In-line skates appear to be 20 percent to 30 percent faster than the traditional quad speed skates, and in-lines are competing in the same races as quads. But because quads are at such a disadvantage against in-lines, the race authorities are now breaking apart these categories. Now, most often, quads race against quads and in-lines against in-lines.

TRAINING FOR RACING

In-line racing is becoming a high-visibility, exciting spectator sport that is attracting sponsorship from major companies around the United States. These sponsorships will help bring the level of competition to new heights and will put increasing performance demands on the sport's top athletes. But this high level of athletic aspiration will appeal to only a small percentage of the skaters, and you can take in-line racing as seriously, or as casually, as you desire. No matter what your chosen level of competition, you can benefit from an organized training program.

ESTABLISHING YOUR GOALS

Having a specific goal, or goals, in mind is the first step toward a good training program. Your goal may be achieving a personal best time for a certain race, or winning your age or skill division.

After establishing your goals, the next step is to develop a training program that will fit into your lifestyle and help you achieve your goals.

SEVEN STEPS TO QUALITY TRAINING

Most people have a full-time job, families, social activities, and hobbies that take time. These interests and responsibilities leave only a small amount of time for training. With that in mind, it's important to recognize that it is the quality of your training that counts, not the quantity.

To achieve the maximum quality from your available training time, divide your training program into the following seven types of training.

FLEXIBILITY

The more flexible you are, the longer and more powerful your strokes will be. Flexibility will also reduce the possibility of muscle injury or strain. The 5 to 10 minutes you devote to stretching is crucial for successful training. For more information on proper stretching exercises, refer to pages 59 to 63 in chapter 3.

CARDIOVASCULAR CONDITIONING

Your cardiovascular system delivers oxygen to your muscles through the blood. The more oxygen you can deliver to the muscles you are using, the faster and longer you will be able to skate. Cardiovascular conditioning—that is, increasing the size of your heart and the amount of blood it can circulate—is one of the most important parts of your training program. The heart, like any other muscle, increases in capacity when used under the proper conditions.

Increased heart volume is achieved by training at approximately 65 percent to 70 percent of the heart's maximum beating rate. This rate is by no means your maximum effort. It is a comfortable pace somewhere between sprinting and leisurely skating. Training at a higher heart rate will increase the heart's speed but not its ability to move larger volumes of blood.

There are several ways to calculate 65 percent of your maximum heart rate, but the simplest is to subtract your age from 220 (which gives you your maximum heart rate) and multiply by .65. A 30-year-old in-line skater who wants to build cardiovascular volume should train at 124 beats per minute ($220 - 30 = 190$; 190 x $.65 = 124$). To measure your heart rate while training, you can use a heart monitor or take your pulse for 6 seconds and then multiply your pulse times 10. Remember that your heart rate can vary depending on your fitness level as well as your natural genetic structure. Because cardiovascular conditioning takes longer to develop than strength and speed, it is recommended that you spend 75 percent to 80 percent of your time on cardiovascular training.

TECHNIQUE

In-line racing is not just a sport of strength and endurance: it is a highly technical sport as well. A proficient racer must use a long stroke (see figure 9.2) and take maximum advantage of the glide between strokes. The glide is actually rest time, enabling a skater whose technique is correct to maintain the same speed as a less proficient skater while using less energy.

FIGURE 9.2 Efficiency, balance, efficiency, coordination, efficiency = SPEED.

The key items to skating correctly are balance, coordination, and efficiency. Stay centered and balanced over your glide skate, take long, fluid strokes, and glide between strokes. Practice and time on your skates is the best way to learn. Focusing on this advice and increasing self-awareness are the best ways to improve your technique.

SPEED

Speed refers to how fast you can move your legs in strokes while still maintaining coordination. You'll use high-speed stroking during starts, breakaways, and sprints to the finish. A few fast, technically correct strokes can increase your speed substantially in a very short distance.

A fast stroke is executed with the snap and explosion of the appropriate muscles, with very little glide time in between strokes, again while maintaining balance and coordination.

139

To practice a fast stroke, work on interval sprints of 1 minute each with a 1-minute rest between sprints. Speed work generally comprises around 10 percent of your overall training regimen. However, as you get closer to race time, you'll want to increase the amount of time you spend with sprint training. You'll want to have strong sprints at both the start and finish of your race and be prepared and well-trained for these parts of the races.

STRENGTH

The more powerful your strokes, the more rest you will be able to take between strokes. As mentioned before, an efficient skater is one who can maintain the race speed while using the least amount of energy.

Building your strength will come from skating up hills or cross-training workouts that put heavier loads on your muscles than skating does. Examples are weight training (see figure 9.3), hiking in the mountains, bicycling in hills, or cross-country skiing. Around 10 percent of your workout should be strength training; however the 6-week program at the end of this chapter devotes even more time to strength training.

RACE STRATEGY

Strategy while racing will vary as the race progresses. A race can be broken down into the start, the pace, the breakaway, and the finish sprint. Strategy appropriate to each of these phases is discussed below. The best way to practice these strategies is to race and skate with groups to simulate races as much as possible.

The Start

The start of a large in-line race can be an intimidating environment for all but the most experienced racers. Approach the start with three objectives:

1. Optimize your starting position. Position yourself in the starting field near other people of similar skill level. If you've been training with other skaters who have similar speed and endurance capabilities, prepare to start around them.

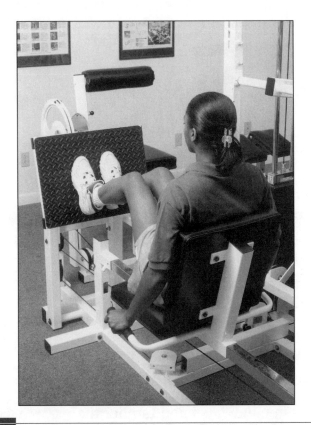

FIGURE 9.3 Weight training can help increase endurance.

2. Strive for a quick start. At the sound of the starting gun, try to get off the line as fast as possible while avoiding other skaters (see figure 9.4). The danger here is getting your legs or skates tangled with a competitor and tripping.

3. Get into a pace line as fast as you can. Pace lines will start to form within 100 yards of the start. It's very important to get into the draft of a pace line as soon as possible to quickly reduce your energy consumption.

The Pace

The most important part of a good strategic race is taking advantage of the draft of other skaters (see figure 9.5). It is difficult for the nonracer to realize how much more efficient you can be while skating in the wind draft of other skaters.

FIGURE 9.4   Lean forward, push off hard, and don't trip!

Research has shown that a racer in a draft can experience a heart rate 20 beats per minute lower while maintaining the same speed.

With this in mind, it is important for the racer to feel comfortable and confident while skating in close proximity to other racers. The key again is practice and training with other skaters. When racing, find a pace line that is skating at a speed that is similar to your desired speed and stick with that line until the final sprint to the finish or a group breakaway.

The Breakaway

There will be times later in the race when some of the skaters in your pace line start to fall back as they tire, and there will be skaters who want to skate faster than the pace line. If you have a desire to pick up the pace, it is best to find other skaters in your pack who will go out with you. Try to pick out the skaters who look strong and ask if they want to go faster. It is very difficult to break away on your own successfully because you won't have anyone to draft on or with. It is important that all skaters involved understand their responsibility to help pull the line.

FIGURE 9.5 Join the pack! This much togetherness takes getting used to, but the draw is the draft—and the camaraderie.

Before making your break, skate back in the existing line for a few minutes so you are well rested. When you break, make it fast and strong to catch the other skaters in the pack off guard. Make a clean break that puts a sufficient amount of distance between you and the previous line so it will be difficult for them to catch up.

The Finish Sprint

Most finish sprints start with a gradual acceleration of the pack and increase to the top speed of the person in front of the pace line (see figure 9.6). Shortly before the finish, individual skaters will break out of the pace line and go for a full-out sprint. In a close race, it's critical to stay in a draft as long as possible to conserve energy. Make your breakaway sprint at the last possible second, allowing yourself enough time to pass the skaters you're trying to beat.

143

© Annelise Cunis

FIGURE 9.6   The finish sprint can decide a race.

REST

Allow a recovery period of 36 to 48 hours after every race or intense workout. Without enough rest, your body won't recover and you will get run down. Fatigue makes you more susceptible to sickness, injury, and burnout, so listen to your body. A tired or sick skater is not a fast one. Get your rest!

You will be stronger in some of these areas and weaker in others. It is best to focus on your areas of weakness. Many of these types of training can be combined into the same workout, and some will require special focus and take longer to develop. For example, it takes a lot more time to develop your cardiovascular capacity than to develop your speed, but you can work on both at the same time.

SIX-MONTH TRAINING PROGRAM

Before starting a 6-month training program, make sure you can skate at a recreational pace for at least one hour. The program covers a normal summer racing season, from April through September, and it is designed so that you will race your best near the end of the season.

Don't worry about overall mileage; distance doesn't tell the whole story. These workouts are structured by time instead of distance so that you can focus on training your aerobic system. By maintaining the target heart rate throughout the workouts, you will gradually skate faster than you did before at the same amount of effort. Try not to time your workouts on the same course, because it's tempting to try to beat your last skate. Remember, stick to the same effort and your speed will take care of itself. If you forget what intensity to skate at, go back to the cardiovascular section earlier in the chapter.

MONTHS 1 THROUGH 3

Objective: To build a strong aerobic base and smooth, stable skating technique.

Workouts: Long skates of 1 to 2 hours, three to four times per week. Start each workout with some stretching, and allow 10 minutes of easy skating for warm-up and 10 minutes for cool-down.

Intensity: Try to maintain 65 percent to 75 percent of your maximum heart rate. This range is fast enough to get a good workout and slow enough to practice proper technique. Look back to Part II to brush up on your skills, and concentrate on long, gliding strokes.

Tips: Work out with people close to your skill level, and practice skating single file in a pace line. Practicing close to others will make you feel more comfortable in races. Avoid racing each other at this point; skating too fast will undermine your training goals. If you don't know many skaters, try a local skate club or ask around at the next race. Most groups welcome new skaters and are eager to share their racing stories.

MONTH 4

Objective: Increase speed and strength. Attend first races of the season.

Workouts: Three skates per week of 30 to 45 minutes and one skate per week that includes hill work to increase leg strength.

Intensity: Move up to 80 percent of maximum heart rate. If you have trouble maintaining proper technique at this intensity, reduce the length of the workout but stick to 80 percent heart rate.

For the hill work, go slowly and stick to the aerobic range of 65 percent to 75 percent if you can. The emphasis should be on your legs, not your lungs.

In addition to the main workouts, allow for a 15-minute warm-up and a 15-minute cool-down at 65 percent of maximum heart rate.

Tips: As in the first three months, continue to skate in a pace line if you get the chance. Once you are comfortable, try to draft (stick close behind) the person in front of you. Drafting will allow you to skate faster with a lot less effort.

Races: Enter up to four 10K races. Try to draft other skaters as much as possible by staying in a pack. If you get left behind by a group, you'll quickly find out how hard it is to catch up skating by yourself. If that happens, don't worry. Try to form another pack, and start chasing! Keep track of your times to measure your improvement.

MONTHS 5 AND 6

Objective: Achieve racing goals and build toward a peak.

Workouts: Skate 45 minutes to 1 hour, two to three times per week. Skate as often as possible with others. Try to push each other to your limits, and practice drafting, passing, breakaways, and lead-ups to sprints at the end of simulated races.

Intensity: Skate as fast as you can while still maintaining proper technique. You will find an intensity level that you can just barely maintain over this amount of time. If you go over it, you have to slow down to recover. For most people it's around 85 percent to 90 percent of maximum heart rate.

Tips: Find your own personal levels of fatigue and recovery. Once you do, you will know how hard you can skate over a given race distance without having to slow down. Be sure to get a full day of rest between workouts.

Races: During the final month, you're ready to race. Before any race, plan on taking it easy for at least five days. If you feel restless, skate at an easy pace (easier than the aerobic pace above) for 20 to 30 minutes on these days. If you have a specific race in mind, try out the 6-week program outlined below. Target your training so the race lands at the end of week 6.

SIX-WEEK TRAINING PROGRAM

Try out this 6-week program any time you want to peak for a race. It will work after the 6-month program, or you can substitute it into the last 6 weeks of your 6-month schedule. If you can't skate for at least 1 hour at a time, however, this program will be too difficult. Work up to this fitness level by skating three to five times a week for as long as you feel comfortable.

This schedule was adapted from a training program by Tony Meibock, a U.S. Olympic speed skater at the Winter Games in

Albertville in 1992. Tony uses the program for both speed skaters (on ice) and in-line skaters.

As you are training, Tony recommends that you take your resting pulse every morning and write it down in a notebook. If your resting pulse suddenly goes up, it's a sign that you're training too much. Back off for a few days and rest, or limit your skating to an easy pace. Monitor your progress with comments for each workout in your notebook. The next time you start a training program, you'll have a personal record of what worked and what didn't. That way you can change the new workouts to fit your body's responses to training.

SKATING WORKOUTS

The biggest change from the 6-month program is the addition of weight training. Research has shown that cross-training with weights can really improve your performance. Stronger muscles translate into faster times. Just try it and see! If you don't have access to weights, substitute another day of aerobic skating or a cross-training activity you enjoy into the weight training days. Swimming, cycling, running, and walking are excellent substitutes. If your legs are stale and sore, take an extra rest day and stick to the skating. Remember, cross-training only supplements your primary training—the best way to get faster is to skate!

Aerobic Skate

As in the 6-month program, aerobic skating is meant to improve your cardiovascular system. The range to shoot for is 65 percent to 75 percent of your maximum heart rate. You should be able to talk and feel reasonably comfortable while you skate. The end of your workout should come because your time is up, not because you can't skate any longer. Remember, skating too fast in these workouts will not give you the same aerobic benefits as sticking within this range.

Long-Interval Skate

Long intervals will help you to improve the pace you can maintain in a race. Start with a gentle 10-minute warm-up skate, and you'll be ready to start the first of five sets. In the first set, skate hard for 2 minutes, rest for 2 minutes, and repeat 3 times. Intensity should range between 80 percent to 90 percent of maximum heart rate. Do three more sets like this, with 5 minutes of rest between sets. For the final set, skate the same workout again, but go as hard as you can in the work interval. Cool down with a 10- to 15-minute easy skate.

Long intervals are prescribed twice in this program, in weeks 3 and 4 (see program schedule, pages 152–153). Use the first workout as a guide for week 4; adjust the workout as necessary. If week 3 was too easy, try increasing the intensity slightly or add a workout to each set (that is, do four repetitions of 2 minutes hard with 2 minutes rest within each set).

Short-Interval Skate

Short intervals are designed to turn your legs over faster than you normally skate. These workouts will help increase your raw speed and stress the limits of your cardiovascular system. Begin with a mellow 10-minute skate warm-up. For the main workout, start with a set of four 60-second interval sprints with 3-minute rests between each 1-minute sprint. Take a 5-minute breather between sets. Second set: five 45-second sprints with 2-minute breaks between each 45-second sprint. Take another 5-minute breather. Third set: six 30-second sprints with 60-second rests between each 30-second sprint. After you've finished all six, take a 5-minute rest. Finish up with seven 30-second sprints with 30-second breaks between each sprint. Call it a day after seven of these.

Tempo Skate

Skate for 5 minutes at as hard a pace as you can maintain. Skate in a low-crouch racing position and give your maximum effort. Allow enough time after your 5-minute skate for full recovery. Your heart rate should return to a resting pulse. Now skate for 4 minutes—again, approximating a race pace. Allow for complete recovery and finish up with one more 4-minute race pace skate.

You'll find two tempo skates in the program, one in week 5 and one in week 6. Since week 6 is race week, use your judgment on how to use the workout. If your legs feel flat, take it easy or skip the workout entirely. If your legs feel fresh, consider it your last hard skate before the race—just don't overdo it! Depending on when your race is, you'll have almost 3 days to recover.

WEIGHT TRAINING

This is a progressive weight-training program, with a different workout for weeks 1 and 2, weeks 3 and 4, and weeks 5 and 6. The correct amount of weight will vary for each person, so don't go by what others are lifting. You should use enough weight that you can just finish the last repetition, but don't sacrifice technique to get there. Err on the side of caution—if you strain a muscle, you may have to stop strength training and rest to get better, which sets back your whole program. Start slowly and work your way up until you get more familiar with what works for you.

Descriptions of the exercises can be found in appendix A on page 184. The first number in the Tempo column is the amount of time you should take to perform the first half of the exercise (for example, lift the weight or squat); the second number is the amount of time you should take to complete the exercise (for example, lower the weight or rise back to the starting position). For example: In the squat the tempo is 3/1. This means you should lower your body in 3 seconds, and then rise back to the starting position in 1 second. For all of the exercises, do not stop in the middle of the exercise. The rest between sets is important—you will gain the most strength in the later sets when your muscles are only partially recovered.

WEEKS 1 AND 2

Exercise	Repetitions (Set 1-2-3)	Tempo	Rest between reps
Squat	15-12-10	3/1	2 minutes
Bench press	15-12-10	1/3	2 minutes
Leg curl	15-12-10	1/3	2 minutes

Pulldown	15-12-10	1/3	2 minutes
Curl	15-12-10	1/3	2 minutes
Shoulder pull	15-12-10	1/3	2 minutes
Leg extension	15-12-10	1/3	2 minutes
Calf raise	20-15	1/1	2 minutes

WEEKS 3 AND 4

Exercise	Repetitions	Tempo	Rest between reps
Squat	12-10-8	2/1	2 minutes
Bench press	12-10-8	1/2	2 minutes
Leg curl	12-10-8	1/2	2 minutes
Pulldown	12-10-8	1/2	2 minutes
Curl	12-10-8	1/2	2 minutes
Shoulder pull	12-10-8	1/2	2 minutes
Leg extension	12-10-8	1/2	2 minutes
Calf raise	12-10	1/1	2 minutes

WEEKS 5 AND 6

Exercise	Repetitions (Set 1-2-3)	Tempo	Rest between reps
Squat	8-6-4	1/1	3 minutes
Bench press	8-6-4	1/1	3 minutes
Leg curl	8-6-4	1/1	3 minutes
Pulldown	8-6-4	1/1	3 minutes
Curl	8-6-4	1/1	3 minutes
Shoulder pull	8-6-4	1/1	3 minutes
Leg extension	8-6-4	1/1	3 minutes
Calf raise	8-6	1/1	3 minutes

PROGRAM SCHEDULE

Here is a day-by-day sample schedule for the 6-week training program. You can model your program after this one or adjust it to fit your specific needs.

After taking a few weeks off (your body will thank you!), you can start the 6-month program or the 6-week program all over again. Use the same intensities outlined above, but this time you'll skate faster at the same level of effort. Don't be afraid to experiment with your training, or to add variety to your workouts.

If you kept a training log the first time through, go back and take a look at what worked and what didn't. Even if you didn't take notes, you should have a better feel for the workouts your body responds to. Remember, structure your workouts so you enjoy them—the most important part of skating is to have fun!

Six-Week Training Program

WEEK 1	Day 1	Day 2	Day 3	Day 4	Day 5	Day 6	Day 7
	SK: A 60 min	WT	SK: A 45 min	R	SK: A 60 min	WT	R

WEEK 2	Day 1	Day 2	Day 3	Day 4	Day 5	Day 6	Day 7
	SK: A 60 min	WT	SK: A 60 min	WT	SK: A 90 min	WT	R

WEEK 3	Day 1	Day 2	Day 3	Day 4	Day 5	Day 6	Day 7
	SK: A 75 min	WT	SK: LI	WT	SK: A 90 min	WT	R

	Day 1	Day 2	Day 3	Day 4	Day 5	Day 6	Day 7
WEEK 4	SK: A 90 min	WT	SK: LI	R	SK: A 60 min	WT or SK: A 45 min	R

	Day 1	Day 2	Day 3	Day 4	Day 5	Day 6	Day 7
WEEK 5	SK: A 60 min	SK: SI	WT	SK: T	R	SK: A 90 min	R

	Day 1	Day 2	Day 3	Day 4	Day 5	Day 6	Day 7
WEEK 6	SK: A 60 min	SK: SI	R	SK: T	R	SK: E 20 to 30 min	RACE DAY!!

Legend:

SK = Skate
WT = Weight training
A = Aerobic
LI = Long interval

SI = Short interval
T = Tempo
E = Easy
R = Rest

CHAPTER 10

AGGRESSIVE SKATING

Courtesy of K2

Let's go! you shout. The weekend is finally here, and your body is full of adrenaline. It's a four-mile skate through deserted streets and sidewalks to the skate park. You can't wait a second longer—you blast off the porch, leaving your friends behind.

The first mile is a warm-up through the neighborhood, but you're going for it early and blast a 360 off the first curb. Soon you hear the crew coming up from behind. They want to catch you before the stairs that drop into the bike trail. You slow a bit and let them blow by, knowing that they'll wait at the bottom of the stairs.

Now, a half-block ahead, they each disappear as they drop down the stairs. You push hard to pick up more speed. Just at the top of the stairs, you compress and then launch, tuck both skates under your body, grab the lower skate, and fly. You land it perfect after 15 steps and keep going down the trail to the skate park.

The park is already crowded. You see two half-pipes, one 12 feet tall with 3 feet of vertical; three quarter-pipes; a spine ramp; a fun box; a 50-foot handrail; and several other small grind rails and ramps.

You spend the day working the vertical of the big half-pipe. It seems to take forever to learn a new trick, falling again and again. And then suddenly it's there: 3 feet above the coping, 15 feet in the air, upside-down, twist, release, perfect landing, smooth transition. You did it! Can't wait to come back tomorrow.

There are two types of aggressive skating, street style and vertical skating. Street skating has developed from urban skaters on the street, using the world as their playground. Vertical skating traces its origin to the pools, half-pipes, and skate parks originally designed for skateboarders.

You will see in-line skaters who can jump cars, grind across a curb, or catch 10 feet of air out of a half-pipe! Like all advanced skating techniques, these maneuvers take a great deal of risk and practice. Analyze each move and the steps that make it work. Wear your safety gear and don't exceed your skill level. Recognize that many tricks take hours, days, and even weeks of practice to learn. Again, learn one small step at a time.

STREET SKATING

In street skating, you use streets, sidewalks, stairs, benches, railings, walls, and other objects as your skate park, executing a variety of tricks and moves on and around these obstacles (see figure 10.1). Just be sure you don't destroy property with any of your tricks! Below you will find an introduction to several basic street moves.

STAIR RIDING

Think of stairs as simply a quick succession of curbs, and you'll understand the basic technique for riding down them

FIGURE 10.1 The street skater creates his own skate park out of what's available in public places.

157

FIGURE 10.2 Stair riding. Stay loose. Keep your stance extended.

(see figure 10.2). If you are comfortable with riding off a curb as described in chapter 8, you're already well on your way to successful stair riding.

The key to riding stairs is maintaining an extended length stance so that both skates do not drop at the same time: The forward skate should drop first and then the back skate. Your knees and ankles will act as shock absorbers as you descend the stairs; stay loose and allow the vibration to be absorbed by your legs.

Your first attempts at stair riding should be done on steps that are slightly wider (deeper) than normal and with less than five total steps; this will allow more time between each drop. As you gain confidence, you can increase the number of steps and the steepness.

GRINDS

A grind is one of the most fundamental moves of aggressive skating. The skater jumps from the regular skating surface

© K2/Scott Markewitz

FIGURE 10.3 Grinding. To come down on the rail in exactly the position you want to grind in—it's tough!

onto the edge of a cement block or railing and slides (grinds) sideways across the surface (see figure 10.3), then lands back on the original surface.

The grinding, in most cases, is done with the frame of the skate (the part holding the wheels onto the boot) sliding across the rail between the middle wheels. Skates should be equipped with grind plates that provide extra strength to the frame to keep it from wearing out quickly or breaking during grinds (see figure 10.4). In some variations of grinds, one of the skate boots is grinding instead of the frame.

Courtesy of Black Hole

FIGURE 10.4 A heavy duty gride plate is necessary to protect the skate frame when grinding.

Learning grinds can be tough. It requires landing with both skates on the rail in the exact position you want to stay in as you grind. It's very difficult to adjust your position once you've started to slide. Practice learning on curbs or rails that are 2 feet from the ground or lower. Falls are part of the price of learning, so wear your safety gear.

Grind Variations

There are many different versions of grinds. Most of them are variations of skate and body position relative to the grinding surface.

● Frontside Grind. When you grind down the rail, you are facing the steps, walkway, or ramp that the rail borders. Approach the rail skating almost parallel to its direction. Just before you reach the rail, jump with both skates and land with a wide stance for stability. Your skates should be perpendicular to the rail, and the rail should be between the center wheels on both skates. Grind down the rail, knees and hips bent, hands in front of your body. As you come to the end of the rail or begin to lose speed, dismount with a slight jump and turn away from the rail in the direction you want to land. Land with an extended length stance.

FIGURE 10.5 Backside grind.

● Backside Grind. When you grind down the rail, your back is to the steps, walkway, or ramp that the rail borders (see figure 10.5). Everything here is the same as the frontside grind except the direction you are facing when grinding. As you jump up to the rail, do a half-turn in the air and land with your back facing the steps or ramp. This landing is more difficult because you can't see the ground as easily. The dismount is the same as a frontside.

● Soul Grind. Your body and front skate face the steps or ramp, as in a frontside grind. The toe of the back skate is turned to face the direction of forward motion, parallel to the rail, and the bottom of the boot is grinding on the rail. The technique is the same as for a frontside grind. Jump onto the rail and land your forward skate as in a frontside. Turn the toe of your back skate in, toward your front skate, and land with the wheels parallel to the rail and the bottom of the boot sliding on top of the rail.

© K2/Darin Back

FIGURE 10.6   Create your own style and grind!

VERTICAL SKATING

Vertical skating may be the ultimate rush on in-line skates. We all remember the childhood feeling of being on a big swing: As we reached the top of the arc, the swing stalled and there was a moment of weightlessness and then a big rush as gravity pulled us back to the bottom of the arc. If you were one of those kids who always wanted to go higher, then vertical skating is for you (see figure 10.7).

The term *vertical*, or *vert*, as used in skating, is a reference to a ramp, empty swimming pool, or skate park that has walls that are straight up and down. The lower part of a ramp that curves from the horizontal ground up to the vertical is called the *transition*. Most ramps are equipped with a railing at the top of the vertical that is called *coping*. Coping is used for grinds, stalls, and other tricks.

Vertical skating works on the same principles as the swing. As a skater skates through the transition from horizontal to vertical, the centrifugal force holds the skater to the wall.

© Hyper Wheels/Taku Taira

FIGURE 10.7 Going vertical. Looks easy enough.

Forward motion gives way to gravity, there is a moment of weightlessness, and then swoosh! Back down the wall, through the transition, and back to the flats! It is slightly before, during, and after the weightless stall that the skater can perform aerial tricks and turns.

GETTING TO VERTICAL

Learning to skate vert takes time and practice. It's a much different feeling than anything you've done on skates before. Vertical skating should only be tried by advanced skaters who feel extremely comfortable and confident on their skates.

163

You will fall when skating on the ramp. Everyone does. When you fall in the transition or from the vert, there is no way to recover except sliding on your body back down the ramp to the flats. Good safety gear is critical. You must wear knee and elbow pads with plastic covers, wrist guards, and a helmet. When you start to fall, tuck your skates under your rear and land and slide on your plastic covered knee pads. If needed, use your elbow pads and wrist guards. The key is to get some plastic between you and the ramp. A good ramp to learn on is one that is quite wide with a flat area below the ramp that is wider than the ramp.

The Transition

Before you ever get up to the vertical, you must master skating the transition. You will see advanced skaters skating straight into and up the ramp. As a beginner, however, the easiest way to learn the feel of skating through a transition is by carving turns through it.

To do this, begin skating toward the ramp at an angle from the side. As you approach the bottom of the transition, set up in an extended length stance. Remember, your forward skate will be the same as the direction you want to turn. Keep your hands out in front and bend your knees. Carve a smooth, wide turn slightly up into the transition from one side of the ramp to the other. Practice this turn from both sides of the ramp, carving both a right and left turn through the transition.

As you get the feel of skating through the transition, you can approach the ramp with slightly greater speed and skate up higher into the transition. The higher you get, the closer to the vertical, the more of a sense of stall or weightlessness you'll feel at the top of the turn. Just before the stall, you can begin to make very small jumps to complete the arc of the turn.

One of the keys to getting higher up the ramp into the vertical is compressing your body at the knees and waist before you enter the transition and then decompressing as you go up through it. Think of your body as a spring coiling tightly and then releasing, or imagine yourself pumping on a swing. With experience, you'll learn to feel that exact moment to hunker down and when to explode out of your compression.

You'll also find that the faster you're going as you approach the transition, the less you need to compress.

Turn at the top and then compress again as you go down through the transition to try for height on the other side.

The Vertical

After you've gained confidence skating up and down through the transition, you'll find more opportunity to learn tricks up on the vertical. The most basic trick is the small jump to complete the turn at the top of your arc (see figure 10.8). At first,

Courtesy of K2

FIGURE 10.8 Jump at top of arc. Okay. NOW you're vertical.

your skates may only come 1 or 2 inches off the ramp, but with practice you will learn to skate higher and make larger jumps.

There are hundreds of types of tricks that can be done on ramps: Hand plants, flips, 360s, grinds, grabs, fakies, and more (see figures 10.9 and 10.10). Learning aggressive vertical maneuvers is a long-term process, so work your way up one move at a time. Practice, watch other skaters, ask questions, and be persistent in your practice.

Courtesy of K2

FIGURE 10.9 It takes hundreds of hours of practice to develop your personal style.

© K2/Chris Slagerman

FIGURE 10.10 Once you've mastered the basic tricks, the possibilities are endless.

Drills

STAIR RIDING

Location: Wide outdoor staircase, no more than four steps, with a clear, flat approach and exit.

1. Wear all safety gear.
2. Begin skating toward top of stairs at slow to medium speed. Approach from an angle.
3. Set up to coast in an extended length stance, hands and arms out in front.
4. Skate down the stairs, legs acting as shock absorbers. Maintain extended length stance.
5. Exit stairs and stop.

FRONTSIDE GRIND

Location: Low cement curb with smooth 90-degree top edge corner.

1. Wear all safety gear.
2. Begin skating toward the curb at a medium speed. Approach from an angle.
3. Just before the curb, prepare for a small jump by compressing at the knees. Keep your hands and arms out in front.
4. Jump up and land on the top edge of the curb. Land with the rail between the two middle wheels, on the curb edge.
5. Grind across the curb edge.
6. Just before you lose forward momentum, jump off the curb and turn your skates forward.
7. Land in an extended length stance and stop.

ROLLER HOCKEY

The roots of modern in-line skating are found in hockey. In the early 1980s, ice hockey players who were looking for a summertime cross-training workout invented modern in-line skates. The popularity of in-line hockey continues to grow at a tremendous pace, with millions of players in school yards around the world. Roller hockey has developed into an independent sport with hundreds of thousands of players who have never played ice hockey.

The popularity of roller hockey has spawned professional roller hockey leagues as well as several organizations to help develop amateur teams and leagues around the world. For additional information on these professional and amateur organizations please refer to appendix B on page 186.

RULES

Roller hockey is based on ice hockey, but the rules of roller hockey are different, making it higher scoring and less dangerous for the players. The National In-Line Hockey Association (see appendix B) has published the *Official Rules of In-Line Hockey* (amateur). The fundamental rules are as follows:

1. The ideal rink size is 185 feet long by 85 feet wide (see figure 11.1).
2. All players are required to wear full safety gear.
3. Each game consists of two 22-minute running time halves (no clock stops) with a 5-minute rest period between halves.
4. Each team consists of four skaters on the rink plus one goalkeeper (five skaters total).
5. There are several types of penalties with varying degrees of consequences. In general, roller hockey follows rules similar to ice hockey but does not allow checking or overly aggressive behavior.

Roller hockey can be played in a variety of places. Parking lots, roller rinks, basketball courts, tennis courts, and out-of-use outdoor ice rinks are the most likely spots. Make sure

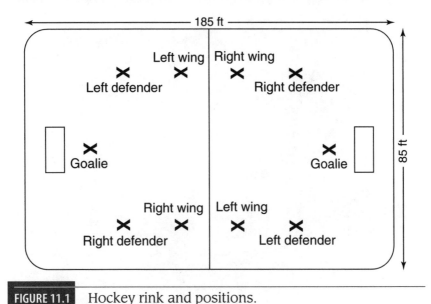

FIGURE 11.1 Hockey rink and positions.

that you are not violating any trespassing rules and keep the skating surface free of dust, dirt, and oil.

HOCKEY GEAR

Playing roller hockey requires some special equipment to withstand the high-impact potential of the sport. In this section, we identify what equipment is important and why.

SKATES

Hockey skates need to be constructed of stiff material to provide maximum support (see figure 2.11 on page 38). The frames should be short, and wheels can be set in a rockered position to allow quick turns and facilitate skating backward. Refer to chapter 2 for additional information on hockey skates (page 37).

PADS

In addition to all normal protective gear as noted in chapter 2, players should also wear padded hockey gloves, shin

© Huron Hockey School

FIGURE 11.2 Hockey players wear additional protective gear.

guards, a mouth guard, and a face cage or shield that attaches to the helmet. In addition, goalies should add heavy-duty shin pads, a chest pad, and a full face cage, and males should wear a protective cup (see figure 11.2).

STICKS

Several styles of roller hockey sticks are available. Many will have a combination of wood and aluminum or wood and plastic (see figure 11.3). Most sticks are designed so the blade

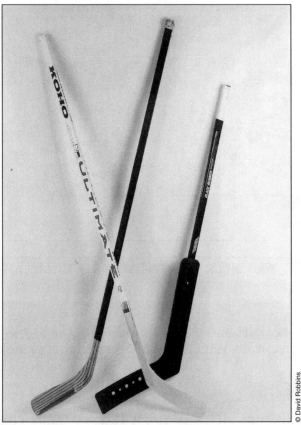

FIGURE 11.3 Different types of hockey sticks.

portion can be removed and replaced with a new blade. The blades wear out quickly when used on cement or asphalt, and buying new blades is less expensive than replacing the whole stick.

PUCK

There is considerable debate among players about the use of a ball versus a puck (see figure 11.4). If you are playing outside on a rough surface, a low-bounce rubber ball designed for roller hockey is preferred. If you are playing on a smooth surface, you can use a puck. There are several different styles

173

© David Robbins

FIGURE 11.4 You can use either a ball or a puck with rollers.

and types of balls and pucks for different playing conditions. A wide selection should be available at most skate shops.

GOALS

Several different styles of roller hockey goals can be purchased, or you can build your own with PVC pipe and netting. Depending on the rules you're using, sizes of nets vary from 3 1/2 by 5 feet to 4 by 6 feet.

BASIC SKILLS

Roller hockey requires special skills above and beyond those of skating. In this section, we review the basics of skating, stick and puck handling, passing, and shooting.

SKATING

Roller hockey players should have a strong set of fundamental skills including quick turns, effective stops, and skating backward. These skills should be instinctive so you can concentrate on the game. Instruction on these skills appears in chapters 4 through 8 of this book.

STICK AND PUCK HANDLING

The hockey stick should be held firmly with both hands (see figure 11.5). Never lift the blade above your shoulders, as this is a violation of the high stick rule and is dangerous to other

© Huron Hockey School

FIGURE 11.5 Hold the hockey stick firmly with both hands.

175

players. When moving the puck, you can cover it by cupping the blade over it and pushing it along or by pushing it side to side with the stick. While controlling the puck, you must keep your head up and watch where you are skating so you will always be prepared to avoid opposing defenders.

To increase your puck handling skills, practice skating through self-made obstacle courses while handling the puck. Your goal is to learn where the puck is and how it will react, even without looking down at it. As your skills increase, you'll be able to fool your competitors. Act as if you are going to move in one direction and then pass, shoot, or skate in the opposite direction.

PASSING

Passing and receiving the puck is an important hockey skill. Be sure that you can handle the puck with both forehand and backhand grips. When passing to a teammate, anticipate the forward movement of the other player and pass to where the player will be when the puck arrives. When receiving or intercepting a pass, allow your stick to move slightly as the puck hits the blade of your stick. This will minimize the chance of the puck bouncing off the stick and your losing control of it.

SHOOTING

Shooting the puck into the goal scores points and wins games. The two most popular shots are the wrist shot, a quick, powerful flick of the wrists that propels the puck off of the blade (see figure 11.6a); and the slap shot, which requires bringing the entire stick back and then swinging it quickly forward so that the blade of the stick contacts the ground a couple of inches behind the puck. This ground contact holds the blade and bends the stick so that when the blade releases, it snaps forward, slapping the puck ahead with great velocity (see figure 11.6b). The wrist shot is usually more accurate than the slap shot but does not make the puck travel as fast.

FIGURE 11.6a The wrist shot is a quick, powerful way to propel the puck off the blade.

FIGURE 11.6a The slap shot allows more speed but less accuracy.

POSITIONS

Each roller hockey team is made up of five players: a goal-keeper, two defenders, and two forwards.

GOALKEEPER

The goalkeeper has perhaps the most challenging job in roller hockey—keeping the puck out of the net at all costs (see figure 11.7). The goalkeeper also has the offensive responsibility of starting the team down the rink with a pass of the puck into play.

The goalkeeper must be able to move side to side quickly in front of the goal, skating both forward and backward. When standing in front of the goal, the goalkeeper should bend at the waist and the knees. Stand so that the side profile blades

© Huron Hockey School

FIGURE 11.7 The goalkeeper wants to keep the puck out of the goal at all costs.

of the skate block as much of the goal as possible. The objective is to block as much of the net as possible from the opponents' view.

The goalkeeper should use any part of her or his body or equipment to stop or deflect shots away from the goal. If the goalkeeper is deflecting a shot, he or she should anticipate the angle of the puck's ricochet and attempt to keep it away from any opposing players.

DEFENDERS

The defender is responsible for trying to stop the incoming plays by the opposing team's forwards. Defenders block shots on their goal, clear the puck from the front of the goal, and move the puck to midcourt and pass it to their forwards to start an offensive play against the other team. Defenders must be able to skate backward to help defend against incoming offensive plays, and they may move up into the attacking territory and assist an offensive play. They often take shots on goal from the point, or the outer corners of the attacking zone near the center line of the rink.

FORWARDS

The forwards are the primary offensive players on their team. They are responsible for moving the puck into the opposing team's territory and setting up plays designed to score goals. Forwards must have good puck handling skills, including passing, faking, and shooting. Forwards must also be in good physical condition, as they skate up and down the rink more than other players. Forwards also take on defensive responsibilities, usually at the beginning of the other team's possession of the puck.

ORGANIZING A TEAM

Check with the skate shops in your area to see if they can put you in contact with other hockey players. Consider organizing your own teams with friends or making up a sign-up sheet to post at your local skate shop to find other players who may be interested in forming a team or league. As you become more familiar with other players in your area, you will be able to put a regular team together and begin to practice together. For more information on forming a team or league, contact one of the hockey organizing groups listed in appendix B on page 186.

Drills

GOALKEEPING

Location: Flat, open, hard rolling surface with a goal at one end.

1. Wear all safety gear.
2. Set up in front of the goal.
3. Have teammates take shots on the goal from various positions on the rink.
4. Block shots with stick, glove, and knee pads.

PUCK HANDLING

Location: Flat, open, hard rolling surface with several obstacles placed randomly.

1. Place hockey ball or puck anywhere on the court.
2. Skate toward the puck.
3. Gain control of the puck with your hockey stick.
4. Skate around obstacles, turning both left and right while maintaining control of the puck.

5. Keep your head and eyes up and looking forward to your next skating direction.

6. As puck handling skills increase, increase skating speed.

PUCK HANDLING TEAM DRILL

Practice this drill as a team. The first skater starts through the course, with consecutive skaters following in close intervals with their own pucks. When a skater loses control of the puck, the skater is out. The last skater in control is the winner.

PASSING

Location: Flat, open, hard rolling surface.

1. Skate side-by-side with another hockey player.
2. Pass the ball or puck to your partner.
3. Receive a pass from your partner.
4. Vary skating speeds.
5. Vary distances of passes.
6. Switch sides to pass and receive with forehand and backhand grips.
7. Place obstacles in the skating area to simulate passing around defenders.

PASSING TEAM DRILL

Practice this drill as a team. Set up with two forwards in the low corners of the rink parallel to the front of the goal and two defenders at the points, forming a square. Practice passing using two pucks around the square and diagonally across the square. Two pucks among four players will sharpen response and handling skills.

SHOOTING

Location: Flat, open, hard rolling surface with a goal at one end.

1. Practice shooting at the goal from various positions.
2. Partially block the front of the goal and shoot at open spots.
3. Vary openings. The most common openings will be the upper and lower corners and the lower middle section.
4. Practice wrist and slap shots from different positions.

SLAP SHOT

Location: Flat, open, hard rolling surface with a goal at one end.

1. Grasp your hockey stick with the lower hand down the stick farther than normal. (See figure 11.6a).
2. Set up with your head over the puck and knees slightly bent.
3. Swing the stick, in a wide arc, back and up.
4. Bring the stick down fast.
5. Begin to shift your weight forward as the blade of the stick contacts the pavement just behind the puck.
6. Complete the weight shift and follow through with the stick swing.

WRIST SHOT

Location: Flat, open, hard rolling surface with a goal at one end.

1. Set your hands on the stick in a normal puck handling position. (See figure 11.6b).
2. Skate toward the goal with the puck controlled against the center of the stick's blade.

3. Cock your wrists back away from the goal.
4. Snap your lower hand forward toward the goal and pull your upper hand back to fire the shot.
5. Follow through with the stick swing and shift your weight forward.

SHOOTING AND GOALKEEPING TEAM DRILL

Set up with the goalkeeper in the net and other players in a line taking consecutive shots at the goal from the same spot on the rink. Vary the shooting position and the type of shots used. Each player should aim for a specific target in the net (for example, the upper right corner).

MORE DRILLS

An excellent source of additional drills as well as tips on every aspect of roller hockey play is *Winning Roller Hockey* by Dave Easter and Vern Stenlund.

WEIGHTLIFTING EXERCISES

Here are the definitions of the weightlifting exercises outlined in chapter 9:

Squat: From a standing position, bend only at the knees into a squatting position until your thighs are parallel to the floor (no farther). Hold dumbbells in both hands by your sides.

Bench press: From a lying position, press a barbell up from the chest, extending your arms fully. Start with very low weights and increase slowly over the 6-week period. *Note:* Never perform this exercise without a spotter!

Leg extension: Using a leg curl exercise machine, from the seated position with your knees bent and the soles of your feet facing the ground, lift the weights forward until your legs are straight and parallel to the ground. Use caution with this and all of these exercises. Start with small weights and work up to heavier weights over the 6-week period.

Pulldown: Using a pulldown machine, kneel on the floor (if necessary) or stand. Start with your arms fully extended above your head. Alternately pull the bar down under your chin and then behind your head to the back of your neck.

Curl: Hold a barbell with an underhand grip, with your arms slightly in front of your thighs so that the bar can clear your body. Keeping your elbows stationary, lift the bar in a curling motion to your chest. Again, start with very light weights. (You may use either a barbell or two dumbbells for this exercise.)

Shoulder pull: Start in the same position as the starting position for the curl, but hold the barbell with an overhand grip. Droop your shoulders to their lowest position, and then raise them toward the sky as far as possible.

Leg curl: You will need to find a proper leg extension machine for this exercise. Lying flat on your belly, slide your feet under the weights. Keeping your belly flat to the surface of the bench, use your leg muscles to raise your feet and bring your heels as close to your rear end as possible.

Calf raise: Place your toes on the top of a slightly elevated platform (3 to 4 inches) with your heels on the ground (below your toes). Carry a barbell as in the starting position for the shoulder pull and raise yourself up on your toes as high as possible.

IN-LINE RESOURCES

The following organizations are excellent resources for additional information on in-line skating.

International In-Line Skating Association (IISA)
3720 Farragut Ave., Ste. 400
Kensington, MD 20895
301-942-9770

International In-Line Skating Association Instructor Certification Program
201 N. Front St., Ste. 306
Wilmington, NC 28401
910-762-7004
(call to find a certified instructor in your area)

United States Amateur Confederation of Roller Skating (USAC/RS)
P.O. Box 6579
Lincoln, NE 68506
402-483-7551

National In-Line Hockey Association (NIHA)
999 Brickell Ave.
9th Floor
Miami, FL 33131
305-358-8988

USA Hockey InLine
4965 N. 30th St.
Colorado Springs, CO 80919
719-599-5500

Aggressive Skaters Association
171 Pier Ave., Ste. 247
Santa Monica, CA 90405
310-399-3436

On the *World Wide Web* see:
Skating The Infobahn
http://www.skatecity.com/
index/

INDEX

Page Numbers in italics are figures.

ABOUT THE AUTHORS

Mark Powell has competed in freestyle skiing, skateboarding, in-line skating, and triathlon events over the last 20-plus years. In 1978 he was the Intermountain Skateboarding Champion. In the first edition of *In-Line Skating*, Powell and co-author John Svensson shared techniques on learning how to in-line skate that were based on the methods used to teach downhill skiing.

Powell is a realtor and freelance writer who has had one other book and numerous magazine articles published. He lives in Redmond, Washington, with his wife Jo. Together they enjoy a variety of outdoor sports.

John Svensson is the director of development for the in-line skating division of K2 Corporation. He began in-line skating in 1979 and has raced for both the Rollerblade and Ultrawheels road teams. He was also a member of the U.S. National Ski Team (Nordic) for six years.

Svensson is a former world record holder for downhill speed on in-lines, having reached a speed of 72 miles per hour on skates he designed and built. His father Einer is a World Masters Cross-Country Ski Champion.

Svensson lives on Vashon Island, off the coast of Seattle, with his wife Yvette and his children, Gunde and Anika.

Techniques, Tactics, and Training

• •

1997 • Paper • 176 pp
Item PNOT0982 • ISBN 0-87322-982-7
$15.95 ($21.95 Canadian)

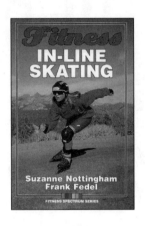

The perfect training guide to help skaters reach their fitness goals, this easy-to-use reference features 48 different workouts grouped across six different training zones of increasing difficulty. Each color-coded zone is designed to challenge skaters in duration and intensity, so skaters can quickly find a workout that fits their needs. *Fitness In-Line Skating* also includes cross-training advice for cycling, ice skating, rowing, running, Alpine skiing, snowboarding, and weight training, and guidelines for using the workouts to design a personal program.

• •

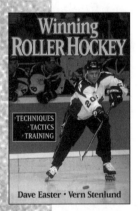

1997 • Paper • 224 pp
Item PEAS0657 • ISBN 0-88011-657-9
$14.95 ($21.95 Canadian)

Expert coaches Dave Easter and Vern Stenlund teach all the important skills and strategies. Sixty-eight practice drills help develop skating, puck control, passing and receiving, and shooting techniques. There's even a special chapter on goaltending! Additional chapters include offensive, defensive, and transition strategies, plus inside tips for competition.

To place your order, U.S. customers call **TOLL FREE 1-800-747-4457**. Customers outside the U.S. place your order using the appropriate telephone number/address shown in the front of this book.

Human Kinetics
The Premier Publisher for Sports & Fitness
http://www.humankinetics.com/   Prices are subject to change.

2335